Lessons from
the Monk I Married

LESSONS

from the

MONK I MARRIED

Katherine Jenkins

SEAL PRESS

"The Voice," by Shel Silverstein is used
by permission of HarperCollins Publishers. Copyright © 1996 EVIL EYE
MUSIC, INC.

Published by Seal Press
A Member of the Perseus Books Group
1700 Fourth Street
Berkeley, California

Library of Congress
Cataloging-in-Publication Data

Jenkins, Katherine, 1969-
Lessons from the monk I married /
by Katherine Jenkins.
p. cm.
ISBN 978-1-58005-368-6
1. Meaning (Psychology) 2. Love.
3. Marriage. I. Title.
BF778.J46 2011
306.872092—dc22
2011009420

9 8 7 6 5 4 3 2 1

Cover and interior design
by Gopa & Ted2, Inc.

Printed in the United States of America
Distributed by Publishers Group West

To my husband,
who has always followed his inner voice—
and by doing so
has helped me find the courage
to follow mine.

Table of Contents

Author's Note

WHILE THIS IS A WORK of nonfiction, most of the names and certain identifying characteristics of the people who appeared along my journey have been changed—with the exception of my family members (because I found it difficult to camouflage them, and after all, my mother is my mother) and my best friend, Lena, who (being that it's hard to camouflage my best friend too) agreed to be named in this book. Seong Yoon Lee, my husband, appears as Su Nim (which means "monk" in Korean) in the first half of the book. He reverts back to his birth name after he leaves the monastery. The city of Sendai, Japan, my home for two years and the backdrop of Lesson Five in this book, was hit by a devastating earthquake and tsunami on March 11, 2011. My heart goes out to all of the people affected by this tragedy, especially to my dear friends and students.

Introduction

THIS BOOK IS CALLED "Lessons from the Monk I Married," but while reading it, you may notice that it would probably be more accurate to call it "Lessons from My Experiences with the Monk I Married."

But I'm not going to change the title. First off, the more "accurate" version doesn't have the right ring to it. Secondly, there is a very clear, if not auspicious, reason why I chose this title for the book, which you will discover in the pages that follow. Lastly, my blog, which now has a fairly large readership, has the same title.

When I started my quest for peace and my life's purpose, I somehow had the belief that I'd find my answers in the pages of self-help books, or in the astrology section of the Sunday paper. True, these did help, and I am very thankful for all the wisdom I acquired from various sources along the way, but I had to make that wisdom my own. If there was one lesson I received from the monk I married—the lesson to top all lessons—it was that I have to walk my own path and find my own wisdom through my own experiences.

It took me a very long time to realize this. I initially believed that wisdom came "from" somewhere else or "from" someone else. Even when this book first took seed, I still believed that the lessons I learned had come from my husband. It was only through writing the book and retracing my steps—which was a journey in and of itself—that I began to see clearly that the lessons I learned came from my own experiences, and that all the people and experiences I encountered along my path merely functioned as mirrors, through which I was able see myself more clearly.

What I also discovered is that it is very easy to surrender ourselves to the laws or rules made up by others without even realizing it. Now, I'm not advocating for people to go out and break the laws set up by society. I'm just saying: Think for yourself. Make your own decisions about what works or what doesn't work in your life.

This doesn't mean that you can't get inspiration from others. Where would our lives be without inspiration? Inspiration from those around us is often what spurs us into action and finally makes us listen to that quiet yet relentless voice inside that's been trying to get our attention all along.

So yes, I believe we can get inspiration "from" others and even learn lessons "from" others—but if we are brave enough to face ourselves, we will find that the adage "You are the one you've been looking for" really rings true. At least that's my experience.

I have practiced Vipassana meditation in the tradition of S. N. Goenka, from India, for more than fifteen years. He is constantly reminding the meditators on his courses this:

> *To witness ultimate truth, you have to remove this curtain of*
> *apparent truth. . . . Direct experience is required.*

He also says that this ultimate truth is the "truth that you experience." Not the truth of anyone else. Still, there will be those within this organization and other organizations that will miss this point completely and have you believe that their laws are the Laws of the Land. This is the point where spirituality gets lost and dogma or religion takes over.

So, with all these lessons I've laid out here in this book, I hope you won't take them as the Laws of the Land. These are lessons I've learned on my journey. This is my story, and I'm sharing it because I've gotten so much inspiration from others along my path. And I hope, by sharing my story, you will be inspired to find your own truth, peace, inspiration, love, and so on. The details of who we are, what we do, and how we live may vary, but the things most of us are looking for on a larger scale—peace, love, a sense of purpose—are ultimately the same.

There are many paths to the top of the mountain, but we all get to enjoy the view if we are willing to keep going, despite all the difficulties we may encounter along the way.

And when you reach the top of your own inner mountain (or mountains), on whatever path suits you, I'd love to hear your story.

Love doesn't have any east or west,

Love doesn't have male or female,

Love is beyond our imagination or fixed mind

of what we think it is,

Love is the source of all beings,

Love is our origin . . . I don't know . . . you know?

Love, love . . . what is love?

—my husband, Seong Yoon Lee

....

Let Go of Expectations

As it is, not as you would like it to be.
—S. N. GOENKA

"LET'S GO BOWLING!" the monk exclaimed, striking his hands together in a clap that simulated thunder. The startling sound broke our in-the-moment-silence and prompted me to drop my metal chopsticks into my *cal guk su* bowl. I looked at my friend Becky, whose eyes widened to the size of quarters. I managed to force a smile and blurt out, "Okay, that sounds . . . nice."

More than six months had passed since Becky and I first arrived in Korea to teach English. And while we'd certainly had our share of amusing experiences during that time, nothing quite compared to this particular afternoon.

It was March 1996, and the trees along the river outside the noodle-hut window were just starting to form buds. Sitting on an *ondul* (heated) floor at a low wooden table, we tried to hone the skill of noodle-slurping while we listened to the monk expound on his recent pilgrimage to Buddhist sites throughout Thailand and India.

A week earlier, Su Nim (which literally translates as "monk" in Korean), had appeared in Becky's free-talking class. She was so intrigued to have this monk show up that she couldn't help but inundate him with questions. Finally, he said, "You seem very interested in monk life. Would you like to have lunch?" It appeared he was inviting her out on a date.

When she told me about it, she asked, "Isn't that taboo?" I had no idea, but I knew I wouldn't be missing *this* adventure. I invited myself along, saying it wouldn't be so taboo if there were three of us.

For days before our meeting, I was giddy with anticipation. I couldn't believe my good fortune: Soon, I would be in the company of a *real live monk*. My reasons for coming to Korea had always eluded me in the past, but now things were getting clearer.

But to explain why this meeting with a monk felt so propitious, I need to take a step or two back.

———

Before I left for Korea, I had been searching for peace.

I'd found some solace in a meditation class at a community college. I'd also found some in books I read while working at an upscale Seattle health club, whittling away the time and handing out towels and locker keys to wealthy patrons in white robes. I'd do my best to disappear behind the counter so that I could settle in, undisturbed, and immerse myself in works such as *Zen Mind, Beginner's Mind*, by the Japanese monk Shunryu Suzuki, who said, "Zen is not some kind of excitement, but concentration on our everyday usual routine."

Boy, was I having difficulty concentrating on my everyday usual routine—which included such exciting tasks as refilling the shampoo in the shower stalls and replenishing the shelves with clean towels. I had to get away.

One day, as I was reading and contemplating how I could make my escape, the club's lifeguard stopped by to tell me she was leaving.

"Good night," I replied, my eyes already back on the page.

"No, I mean I am *really* leaving," she said. "I'm going to South Korea next week. My boyfriend got a job there. I guess this is it." And with that, she disappeared through the door, leaving me alone in the club. I found myself feeling more alone than I had in months, and save for the buzz of the florescent lights, the club was eerily silent. As I sat frozen at my towel desk, I had the urge to run after her, but it was too late.

All the way to the bus stop that night, Korea wouldn't leave my mind. She sat next to me on the bus and followed me home. She lay next to me in bed as I stared wide-eyed at the ceiling. She kept me awake for most of the night. I didn't know much about Korea, but there was a familiarity about her that I couldn't quite place. I'd say to her, "Have we met?" And she would smile, shake her head politely, and disappear into the crowd.

At the end of summer, I quit my job at the health club and went on an extended road trip with my mother across the United States. I continued reading everything and anything I could get my hands on that might help me find the inner peace I was searching for. I started with Zen and ended with American Transcendentalism, including *Walden* by Henry David Thoreau, prompting a side trip to Walden Pond.

After nearly three months on the road together, my mom was ready to go home. But I just couldn't bear the thought of going with her, of living at home. I had graduated from college three years earlier—I needed a life, and quick! So I went to live with my college boyfriend in Tacoma, Washington, instead. I got a job as a teaching assistant at a K–12 Christian school. I wasn't sure how that fit in with all the Buddhist and Transcendentalist reading I was doing, but by this point, I couldn't be picky.

One afternoon, as I wiped down the lunch tables, picking up pieces of half-devoured food scraps from the floor, I had a distinct thought: *Is this it?* Many of my college friends had already settled into career paths and lives with their partners. *Should I be settling down, too?*

Settle down.

Those two little words made me cringe. It was just, well, so final—and too boring. But my current job and living set-up weren't working for me, either.

But time went by and it appeared that settling down was exactly what I was doing. Until one night while driving to dinner, our mutual friend Mike announced to my boyfriend and me, "I think I'm going to go teach English in Korea."

My mouth opened and formed a silent *What?* I had suddenly gone mute.

Mike continued. "Yeah, you know, Brian is over there. They have a couple openings for teaching positions at the school where he works."

I found my voice again. "Uh, could you let him know I'm interested?"

My boyfriend's glare seemed to say, *Oh, great. Here she goes again.*

And then the conversation shifted to something else. I have no idea what the topic was; I was staring out the window of the car, once again lost in the word *Korea.* I was in a daze most of the evening, and my boyfriend sensed that something was brewing. He knew I wasn't happy where I was, and that it wouldn't be long before I left . . . again.

Leaving had become my habit. During my junior year in college, I left him to study abroad in Spain, and later, after we graduated, I ventured down to Mexico to teach English. There, I saved enough money to travel to Peru and Bolivia on my own. The doubts I had about settling down were always replaced by larger, more esoteric questions while traveling. For example: "Should I get married?" morphed into "Why am I here on this planet?" Perhaps the absence of societal pressures on the road allowed space for more existential questions to surface. Whatever the case, I felt the itch to go.

My boyfriend and I never broke up while I was off on my sojourns to different parts of the globe, but perhaps we should have. Instead, we always managed to pick things right back up after I returned home, but I know it hurt him that I couldn't stay put and committed to only him. The truth is, I found it difficult to be committed to anything, including my direction in life. On the road, I didn't need a direction. I was free to choose a different course every day. In each new place I visited, I allowed myself to experience and explore the country and culture fully—and that included relationships, when the occasion arose.

A few days later, Brian called and filled me in on the details of the job. I don't know if I really heard any of what he had to say, but at the end of the conversation, he said, "So, do you think you want the job?"

"Yes." The word popped out of my mouth before I had time to think about it. It was out of my hands: I was going, and that was that.

———

When I boarded the plane for Korea in August 1995, I was only twenty-five. There was still so much I wanted to know, to feel, and to see. I wanted to travel to the remotest locations, both in the world outside and within my own inner world. I was ready to fully explore and answer those bigger questions: *Who am I? Why am I here?*

What is my purpose in life? On the plane, I felt a vastness I can't fully describe. It was like I had become the entire, endless sky that surrounded the airplane. I felt suspended above time and space. I felt everything and nothing. I felt an emptiness that was full.

As the plane started to descend, I could barely make out the landscape below me, but I envisioned it full of ornate temples and friendly people riding bicycles with baskets and bells. I had a feeling that I was going to experience something magical.

All of my expectations were shattered, however, when I arrived to the sweltering August heat of a rural airport in Pohang, in southeastern Korea, near the East Sea.

Mike had arrived there a few weeks before me, so he and his girlfriend, Karen, along with Brian, met me at the airport. After collecting my luggage, we boarded a bus to Gyeongju, one hour north. I spent the entire trip looking out the window and did not see a single bicycle the whole way.

Or a temple, for that matter.

What I did see were cars zipping through the streets, disobeying any kind of traffic sign. There was so much concrete and so few trees along the highway as we approached our destination. Everything looked barren in comparison to the Evergreen State I called home.

My friends dropped me off at a room in an old building; they had a different living situation than mine. I examined my accommodations. There were bars on the window, and the shared toilet down the hall was broken. (Considering that I now had a bad case of diarrhea, most likely from the nervousness and excitement I felt upon arriving in Korea, this was a predicament.) I sat on the toilet and watched cockroaches scurry across the concrete floor as I contemplated how I would flush. Then it dawned on me that the bucket on the floor was there for a reason. Besides the non-functioning toilet, there was no air conditioner or fan to speak of, so I didn't sleep much that night. Instead, I lay awake for hours in a sweat staring at the ceiling, wondering what on earth I was doing here.

In the weeks that followed, I learned that I would be moved from my prison-like cell to a "love hotel." I wasn't sure if this was a move up or down from my present digs. The new room was a bit bigger, with a functioning private bathroom attached, but the situation was hardly ideal. First of all, I would be living in a hotel. Second, it leaned more towards the "red light" variety than a Holiday Inn.

While it occurred to me that Korea might be exotic, this was not really what I had in mind. I preferred my old broken toilet to my present one—which worked, but had a huge AIDS sticker above the toilet paper roll, clearly placed there as a warning to patrons in the basement who sang karaoke alongside women of the night. I assumed the empty rooms were used for whatever followed, though thankfully, I was never disturbed by any strange sounds from guests who ventured upstairs.

My school had moved the teachers to this new locale because the monthly rent was cheap, but it was certainly *not* how I had pictured my living situation in Korea. Prior to my arrival, I had imagined I'd be placed in a little temple-like dwelling with a slanted roof and paper-thin sliding doors. I'd sleep on the floor and have a cozy little stove upon which I'd boil water for tea on cold nights. I'd listen to the sound of crickets and cicada in the summer and watch snow fall outside my window in the winter.

Not only did I not have a stove, I didn't even have a kitchen. For an entire year, I ate out every day. Instead of hearing the sounds of the great outdoors, I heard karaoke music and drunken Korean businessmen. While I never learned to call the place home, by the time the chill of fall set in, I reluctantly learned to accept my conditions.

Luckily, by then, Becky had arrived.

Like me, Becky had been hired to teach English at Sisa Foreign Language Institute, near downtown Gyeongju. Fate had thrown us together, and since she was the only other foreign woman living in my building, we bonded out of the sheer need to survive in our new environment.

We were from opposite ends of the spectrum—geographically, physically, and psychologically. She was from Halifax, in northeastern Canada. I myself am a West Coast gal, having grown up in Bellevue, Washington. She had dirty blond hair, dark brown eyes, and dimples. I have blue eyes, dark brown hair, and freckles. Becky laughed whenever she was nervous (which was quite often, especially when she first arrived). I tend to rely on my intuition, particularly in new settings, and have a contemplative nature.

Despite our differences, however, we shared one thing in common: a sense of humor.

"Um, do you know why my room doesn't have any windows?" she asked me. She had just arrived and was obviously taken aback by her new pad. She was hunched up on the corner of the bed, arms wrapped around her knees, suitcase splayed out on the floor.

"I think you got one of the defective rooms," I replied.

She looked over at me and laughed. "What am I *doing* here?!"

That was the moment I knew we'd be friends—I had asked myself the very same question upon arrival and every night after that.

I gave her the lowdown on what I knew of the school and the city while she showed me some of the gifts she brought from Canada for the school staff. There were jars of jam, calendars with pictures of Canadian scenery, and other trinkets.

From that point on, Becky was present on many of my early adventures in Korea—including our first date with a monk.

It helped that her room was just down the hall from mine, as it allowed me the opportunity to stop by any chance I got to talk and for both of us to share our new experiences. In many instances, humor helped us to soften the blow of culture shock and to deal with uncomfortable situations. Like the day another foreign woman moved in.

"Where are you teaching?" I asked the new arrival, hoping there would now be three of us to shoot the breeze about the craziness of our living situation.

"Oh, I'm not a teacher," she replied, smiling. She had a foreign accent I couldn't immediately place.

"You're not?" I questioned, eyeing Becky.

"No, I'm a dancer. I'm only here for a few weeks, just to earn a bit of money."

Hesitant to ask any further questions, Becky and I kindly excused ourselves for lunch. The woman barely noticed our exit; she didn't seem too interested in making friends on her short stopover.

Later on, I said to Becky, "Maybe the school really hired us to be dancers. Maybe that's why we live in the love hotel."

Becky nearly choked on her food in a burst of laughter. After that, she made me promise not to make any more jokes while we were eating.

So here we were, two English teachers living among exotic dancers and their patrons. But no one ever bothered us, so we carried on with our lives. We walked to school, ate meals out, and visited historical places around the city on the weekends. I was happy to find that Korea *did* contain the ornate temples I had imagined, but it was not the bicycle-friendly country I dreamed it would be.

But as much as I started to get used to my life in Korea, nothing earth-shattering had happened. With all the signs pointing me here, I thought for sure that I would discover something new about myself. But much to my growing disappointment, the scenery was all that had really changed.

That's why I was so excited when, seven months into my time

in Korea, I found myself having lunch with a real live monk. I felt certain that sharing lunch with Becky and the monk that afternoon would finally shed light on all my unanswered questions—including why I was in Korea, and how I could find the elusive peace I felt like I'd been looking for my entire life.

———

I just never expected my search for peace would lead me to a bowling alley. Nor did I expect my first experience with a Buddhist monk to involve putting on tacky shoes and comparing ball sizes. No—I expected we'd spend the afternoon watching monks chanting and doing prostrations to the steady beat of a *moktak*, a wooden percussion instrument used in Korean Buddhist ceremonies. Or maybe we'd attend a tea ceremony, sitting for hours on our knees in silence. Or maybe I'd even finally learn how to meditate.

Yet here we were, following Su Nim through the narrow streets downtown to the bowling alley. Along the way, I started worrying. *Is there a certain etiquette I should follow when bowling with a monk?* I wondered. *No, that's ridiculous. How could there be an etiquette? Who goes bowling with a monk, anyway?*

Inside the bowling alley, Su Nim took off his long gray robe, revealing a T-shirt over which he wore the most unusual gray patchwork vest. It was stitched together with squares of hand-dyed Korean cloth that varied in hue and texture. I couldn't help but stare at its uniqueness as he sat down to tie his bowling shoes.

"I used to be on a bowling team," he announced with a childlike smile. "I had my *own* shoes then."

He used to be on a bowling team? What were we getting ourselves into? I didn't even like bowling, nor was I good at it. I glanced at Becky to see what she thought of all this. She just raised her eyebrows at me and shrugged, as if to say, "Just go with it." So I did. I swung my arm back, let go of my ball, and watched it roll straight into the gutter. Embarrassed, I hurried back to a vacant bench, anxious for the next bowler to step up to the lane as soon as possible, hoping that no one would comment on my lousy performance.

While I attempted to disappear, Su Nim stood out in more ways than one. Running down the lane in his gray, poofy pants, patchwork vest, and white T-shirt, his bald head as shiny as the ball he held to his chest, he looked like a star bowler, except for the unusual get-up. He made a number of strikes that afternoon, shouting out "Oh, *yessssss!*" after each one and pulling down his clenched fist in a manner usually reserved for rock stars. Then he'd run over to each of us and give us a high-five.

He whipped Becky and me in every game.

As we were leaving, Su Nim suggested we visit a teahouse downtown. *Finally*, I thought. I was worried that my only experience out with a monk would begin and end in a bowling alley. On our way there, we learned that Su Nim lived a temple above the teahouse in a room adjacent to a meditation hall. People from town would gather in the hall in the early morning for meditation sessions guided by Su

Nim. As it turned out, the teahouse he was taking us to was not just a teahouse, but *his* house and place of work. Things were looking up.

When we arrived, I was overcome by an immediate sense of calm. Su Nim invited us to sit on wooden stools around a wooden table. Traditional music wafted through the air as we sipped from tiny porcelain cups of green tea. *This is more like it*, I thought.

After many rounds of tea, Su Nim realized he'd left his book at the bowling alley. Since it was near the love hotel, I volunteered to retrieve it. Feeling tired from our long day, Becky went home ahead of me and I returned to the bowling alley. I found the book on a bench near our lane. To my surprise, it wasn't a sacred text of Buddhism as I imagined it would be. It was *The Discipline of Transcendence*, by Osho.

Osho? I thought. *Wasn't he the same guy as Bhagwan Shree Rajneesh, the guru who had the fleet of Rolls Royces? Who talked about "free love"? Who started a commune in Oregon?*

I couldn't believe that a monk would be reading a book by such a controversial figure, but the more I thought about it, I realized there was little that was traditional about Su Nim. Clearly, this monk moved to the beat of his own *moktak*.

On the walk back to the love hotel, I reviewed my day out with the monk and found I had more questions now than answers. I tried to believe I wouldn't let my curiosity get the better of me, that I wouldn't pry, that I wouldn't open the book when I got home, that I'd just leave it in my handbag until the next day. But that was not going to happen. I wanted to know more.

The large neon sign marking my love hotel lit up the sky like fireworks on the Fourth of July, and off-key karaoke music blared into the parking lot. In the lobby, the owner sat at the front desk, his nose in a newspaper. I climbed the stairs to my third-floor room and walked down the hallway feeling claustrophobic. The place I thought I had finally gotten used to suddenly felt foreign again. I unlocked the door, took off my shoes, and sat down on the edge of the bed, my bag in my lap, waiting for some divine intervention to give me an answer as to what I should do.

Nothing.

I grabbed the book out of my bag and held it in my hands. And then I opened it. The first thing I saw was a yellow piece of paper Su Nim must have tucked inside the pages, with some English words written on it.

Take it easy, everything is okay.

The next thing I noticed was that he'd underlined some passages.

The way can only be known if you deeply participate with existence. It cannot be known from the outside, you have to become a participant. . . . Meditation is something that is happening in [your] very being, deep inside. You cannot observe it, there cannot be any objective knowledge about it.

The passages ignited an understanding of something I was attempting to figure out. I had spent so much of my past being concerned about what people thought of me, and trying to conform to those expectations. By setting out on this journey to Korea, I was hoping to find out who I was, apart from the societal roles I'd been playing.

But even in this new environment, far from my family members and peers, I was still a victim of my *own* expectations—expectations of others and of myself. I still governed my life by what I deemed important from an *outward* view. An inside perspective of who I was did not exist for me yet, nor did I know how to see my life from that vantage point.

I was both confused and fascinated by Su Nim—confused because he didn't live up to my expectations of how a monk should be, and fascinated because he apparently understood enough about himself not to care what others thought of him.

It was clear that in my quest to learn about myself, I still had a long way to go. But it was also clear that my afternoon out with this intriguing monk was step in the right direction. He was evidently someone who understood the "inside" part—the part I desperately wanted access to. The part that so eluded me when I'd attempted meditation in the past.

The next day, when I saw Su Nim at the language institute, I asked him about joining the meditation sessions in the temple above the teahouse we'd been to.

"I will ask the temple master and let you know," he replied.

I waited two days with no response and was beginning to feel a bit dejected, like I was somehow unfit for these meditation sessions. Finally, before joining his English class one afternoon, he turned to me and said, "Kathy, if you want to study meditation at the temple, you are welcome. Congratulations!"

Congratulations? It was not the response I was anticipating, but again, there was nothing about Su Nim or Korea, for that matter, that had ever been predictable.

So, for several months, I groggily woke at three-thirty in the morning and rode my bicycle through the city streets to the temple, passing drunks yelling and stumbling down the road. I'd try to keep myself steady and awake on my bike, all the time wondering what the hell I was doing riding my bike through the city at this hour. Had I lost my mind?

And then I'd arrive at the temple above the teashop and forget all those thoughts and feelings. I loved the peacefulness and the smell of incense that greeted me as I entered the meditation hall.

Su Nim led each ceremony by hitting a large bell three times. Then, he'd chant sutras while hitting a *moktak* and doing prostrations. After the chanting was finished, we'd meditate for fifty minutes, walk in a circle for ten minutes, and then meditate again for fifty minutes.

While I loved the ambiance of the temple, the meditation was difficult for me. Add to that the fact that it was so early in the morning, and that I never ate before sitting. I was so afraid my growling stomach would disrupt the other meditators—Koreans who, unlike me, appeared to be sitting unflinchingly in a state of complete meditative bliss.

We were never given any instruction on how to meditate, other than to sit with a straight back and neck, and to keep our eyes half-opened. I kept thinking I would see divine light, or an angel or something. But without my glasses, I only saw undefined shapes. I wanted to feel the bliss everyone else looked like they were experiencing, but the only things I felt were "the monster" in my belly and painful knees.

Becky joined me for several weeks in the beginning. Since we were both new to meditation, we had lots of questions for Su Nim—and luckily, Su Nim had lots of patience for us. One day, after a session, I asked him what we should do when thoughts arose. He looked and Becky and me and said, "Your thoughts are just like fish in the ocean. Leave them alone. The ocean is much bigger than your thoughts."

Later that day, I asked Becky how she was feeling about the meditation sessions. Exhausted, she said, "I think all my fish have died and are floating on the surface of the ocean."

I laughed and congratulated her, joking that if her fish had died, then surely that meant her thoughts had died—and wasn't that the point? But she just looked at me, puzzled. She wasn't laughing. That was the last time Becky would attend the early-morning sessions.

I had to admit it: These sessions were making me a bit delirious too. I felt tired in my language classes, but I tried to keep going anyway. I still had so many questions about meditation—too many to ask Su Nim comfortably in person. And so I decided to write them all down.

> *Can you tell me what to do when I meditate?*
> *Do I sit and watch the mind?*
> *Do I focus on an object?*
> *Do I concentrate on breathing?*
> *What do you do when thoughts come to you?*
> *Do you have any special experience, or are you just sitting and aware?*

And one day, as he was about to descend the stairs after a session, I whipped out the list from my pocket and placed it in Su Nim's hands. He smiled a warm, affectionate smile; took the piece of paper from my hands; and then turned and left.

Two days later, after meditation, Su Nim handed me back a folded note containing my original questions followed by his reply, in neat script.

> *Korean traditional meditation manners are somewhat different than Western meditation. Some recommend you focus on an object or concentrate on breathing and so on. But if you want real spiritual development, you need three things. First, great faith in yourself (you are a Buddha). Second, you have to doubt (What am I? Or, what is it?). Third, you need concentration of mind continually.*

His words did not sink in for a long time, but I didn't give up on the meditation. I continued to wake up at an ungodly hour to attend those sessions. Day after day, I shakily steered my bicycle through darkness toward the soft, flickering candlelight of the meditation room. I sat through pain, uneasiness, restlessness, and sheer boredom.

And then, one morning, something happened.

I started to feel myself as I was. I was able to let go of my expectations of how I thought I should feel and just felt.

After that session, I wasn't lost in my usual cloudy haze. I was alert. I felt the blood pulsing in my veins as I pumped my bicycle pedals toward home. As I rode, the sun started to make its appearance on the horizon, casting a warm glow across the sky and onto my face. I felt a deep, euphoric calm.

I asked Su Nim about these experiences. "Don't give them any importance," he said flatly.

Now I was really confused. I wanted confirmation that I had finally achieved something. I'd expected something more along the lines of, "Good job! Way to go!"

"Everything changes," Su Nim continued. "Learn to accept things as they are and keep your awareness in every moment; then you will understand about meditation."

His words awoke something in me—a fundamental truth I had failed to recognize previously, but which was starting to make itself clear now: things change and there's nothing to hold onto.

All these expectations I'd had—expectations of how my life

should be, how Korea should be, how a monk should be, how I should be—were just that: expectations. They were not reality, as the reality of each moment is constantly changing.

I wanted to hold onto this new awareness. I wanted to put in my back pocket and carry it with me everywhere I went, but just like everything else, it was fleeting and only made its appearance when I wasn't trying to capture it. The only thing I could do was to accept things as they were, but this was going to be a challenge.

....

There Is No Such Thing
as a Meaningless Coincidence

If the time is right, we will meet the people
we are supposed to meet.
—SEONG YOON LEE

FIVE MONTHS BEFORE I'd first met Su Nim, I was sitting on my love-hotel bed, leafing through my Lonely Planet guidebook to Korea. Suddenly, on page 240, on the top right-hand side of the page, something popped out and grabbed my attention: Songgwang Temple.

According to the guidebook, it was a famous training center for novice monks who came not only from Korea, but from other countries as well. Two lines down in the description, the words "three jewels" caught my attention. Drawing upon my limited knowledge of Buddhism, I realized that must be another name for the "Triple Gem"—the Buddha (Enlightened One), the Dharma (the teachings of an Enlightened One), and the Sangha (those who are following this teaching). And I was right: Songgwang Temple, as it turns out, is one of three Korean "jewel" temples, representing the Sangha in South Korea.

I'd only just recently arrived in Korea, and I'd yet to meet any practicing Buddhists, let alone monks. But oh, how I wanted to meet a member of the Sangha! If not at Songgwang Temple, then where? I told Becky about my plans to go.

"Songgwang Temple?" she said, plopping down on my bed. "Where's that?"

I showed her the map and pictures in my guidebook.

"I don't know, it seems so far away," she concluded.

"I know," I said, closing my book and looking out the window. "But I just have this feeling that I have to go there." I wasn't sure, however, if I wanted to go it alone. Becky was right; it was far. And Korea was still so new to me. But as usual, my curiosity got the better of me.

After work one Friday in early October, I made a beeline to my hotel. I'd made my decision. I was going, and I no longer cared that it was far away, or that most of my weekend time would be spent traveling to get there. Usually, on Friday night, I would go out with fellow teachers after work at around nine to eat, play pool, drink, and sing karaoke, but not this time. I stuffed some clothes, toiletries, and money into a small backpack and set it by the door.

The next morning, I woke up at five, grabbed my backpack, and headed out into the chilly morning toward the station where

Korean *ajuma* (older, married women) squatted in front of a line of buses selling *bundegi* (boiled silk worm larvae), tangerines, and canned drinks. Food was the last thing on my mind, however, as I wove through the crowd to the ticket counter. I was too anxious about the journey to be hungry.

I didn't speak the language very well, and it was my first solo trip outside of Gyeongju. I was nervous about how I'd make all the bus transfers—and if I'd even know whether I was on the right bus. At the ticket counter, I hesitantly sputtered "Busan"—the name of my first stop—and hoped the elderly agent would be able to decipher my pronunciation. From Gyeongju, it would take me six hours and three buses to arrive at my destination.

When I finally got to the temple, it was nearly two in the afternoon. Slanted roofs with curved dark-gray stone tiles graced the tops of the temple buildings. They looked like coats of armor, protecting all that was inside. On the overlapping hills behind the temple grounds, bursts of gold leaves from maples peeked out between the pine trees of a dense forest, creating a striking contrast. Dusty gravel stretched out in front of the temple. Nothing grew in this space; it was a space of emptiness.

This emptiness sent a shiver down my spine. It was a beautiful place, but it felt a like a ghost town.

Where were the monks?

Where were the tourists?

Where were the people who dusted off the statues of the Buddha?

I took off my shoes and entered one of the temple buildings. A large golden statue of the Buddha sat against the far wall, and the smell of incense permeated the air. Turquoise, brown, red, and yellow mandalas and geometric patterns adorned the ceilings, and on the walls were paintings that depicted the life of the Buddha. A big red cushion sat on the dark wooden floor in front of the Buddha, and a table in front of the cushion displayed a book of sutras and a *moktak*.

Taking a silk cushion from the stack by the door and placing it on the floor, I joined my hands in *namaste*. Bending at the waist, I came down on my knees and folded my body forward, placing my head on the cushion. From there, I slowly rose to standing position, and then repeated this sequence two more times. And then I closed my eyes and sat there in silence for a few minutes. A breeze blew through the side door where a wind chime's melody seemed to speak to me, calling me to venture outside.

I arose and exited the temple, wandered around the grounds, took a couple of pictures, and then walked down a dusty trail toward a river. As I walked farther down the path into the woods, the loud river gushing past me made all other sounds inaudible. At every twist and turn along the way, I kept hoping I'd find a wise, old monk or temple master sitting along the river's edge, ready to give me the answers to all my questions. (Not the least of which was *Why had I come to this temple?* And *Why had I come to Korea in the first place?* I thought someone who had been practicing the teachings of the Buddha ardently might have more insight than I did about why I was there.)

But I didn't meet a soul.

Before leaving, I took one last photo of the main temple. Standing among several other tourists, I raised my camera and looked through the lens. At that exact moment, a line of monks wearing long gray robes and brown ceremonial sashes emerged from a large door. They were in single file, and they kept an even pace and an equal distance between each other, focusing on each step. Walking slowly to another building in the complex, the monks covered their faces with their hands or sleeves, not interested in making eye contact with any onlookers. I focused on the procession through my lens and took the picture, and then headed back to the station.

Back in Gyeongju, memories of my trip to Songgwang Temple faded into the distance almost immediately. I got up early on Monday, took a shower, and ate breakfast. On the way out, I knocked on Becky's door hoping she'd walk to school with me, but she had already left. She'd been gone all weekend too. I was in a hurry, as usual, and walked quickly. I still needed to get some photocopies made in time for my nine o'clock class.

As soon as Becky saw me, she strode straight over to the copy machine. "So, how was it?"

"It was all right," I mumbled. "Just another temple."

A month after our bowling adventure, Su Nim and I began to meet for tea regularly, and during these meetings, we'd talk about my questions, the big ones I'd hoped I'd find answers to while in Korea. I was interested in getting a Buddhist perspective on these questions, and he was happy to be of service in my quest for answers. Since teahouses were plentiful in Gyeongju, on each of our outings we'd visit different ones, and it wasn't long before I knew them all.

One of my favorites was in a split-level building. On the first floor, there were tables, chairs, a kitchen, and a reception area, and upstairs, patrons could sit on a tatami floor around low wooden tables, enjoying a bit more seclusion. One day we returned to this teahouse and climbed the stairs to the second level. The room was empty. We each picked up a brightly colored cushion from a stack in a corner and placed them on the floor. As we were about to sit down, the waitress came upstairs and took our order.

"*Nok cha chuseyo*," Su Nim said. ("We'll have green tea.")

And she disappeared down the stairs. We were alone.

The monk lifted up the back of his thick, long gray robe to sit down. I sat across from him and watched while he folded his hands on the table and smiled at me. We sat in silence.

After a minute or so, I pulled a photo album out of my backpack. I thought he'd be interested in seeing pictures of the temple I visited when I first arrived in Korea. Perhaps he could shed more light on the significance of Songgwang temple from a Buddhist standpoint. Or maybe he could reveal why I was so drawn to the place right off the bat. Maybe the temple had some supernatural force that drew visitors from all over the globe. I had heard about people in Europe and the Middle East setting out on foot for weeklong pilgrimages to holy sites. So I imagined there must be places like that in Korea.

I passed the album to him over the tea table. "Here are some pictures from my visit to Songgwang Temple in early October."

His eyes flashed up and met mine. It was as if he were recalling something, and he seemed startled. He opened the album's front cover slowly and looked down at the first few photos, pausing before turning the page. Then he caught my eye again and smiled a half-smile. When he turned to the third page, he just sat there, staring at the pictures for a very long time.

I didn't understand. There wasn't anything *that* interesting in the album. There were just photos of the temple complex and the grounds surrounding it. I sat up on my knees to get a closer look at what he was staring at for so long. It was the procession of monks coming out of the temple door—the last photo I had taken before I left that day.

"That's me," he said, pointing to the lineup.

I moved around to his side of the table and crouched down to look. As I'd remembered, most of the monks in the procession had covered their faces or were looking at the ground as they walked to the left toward another door in the complex. But one monk, the last one in line, had raised his head slightly and was faced toward the camera when I took my photo. He hesitated there for a few seconds before turning and joining the other monks. That monk was Su Nim.

I couldn't believe it. I sat speechless on the floor, staring at the photo for several minutes. Finally, I said, "What a coincidence."

"No, it's not," he said. "If the time is right, we will meet the people we are supposed to meet."

And with those words, I realized something that took my breath away: All of my searching had led me *here*. All those days in the health club, thumbing through book after book on Buddhism and meditation—those days had a purpose. The lifeguard who first got me thinking about Korea; that night with Mike, when I first learned of the teaching opportunity—they were not just coincidences. All along my journey, my intentions had been connecting me to the right people and the right places. My sincere wish to meet a monk on my journey to Songgwang Temple *hadn't* gone unheard: I *had* met a monk from the temple. (Albeit, he loved to bowl, had a funky patchwork vest, and liked to read books by Osho, but he was a monk, nonetheless.)

Though little had unfolded as I expected it to, these were not random events in a chaotic universe. For the first time in my life, I was aware that my intentions were creating my connections. And that I was right where I needed to be.

....

Trust Your Inner Voice

There is a voice inside of you
That whispers all day long,
"I feel that this is right for me, I know that this is wrong."
No teacher, preacher, parent, friend
Or wise man can decide
What's right for you—just listen to
The voice that speaks inside.

—"THE VOICE," BY SHEL SILVERSTEIN

IT WAS RAINING, spring was in the air, and April was far upon us. My teahouse meetings with Su Nim had become a ritual, and I looked forward to our get-togethers more than any other part of my week.

While most of the teahouses in town usually had plenty of customers, we found ourselves completely alone one day; not even the shop owner was in sight. It wasn't the first time we'd drank tea alone, but there had always been an employee or two clamoring in the background to remind us that no, we weren't the only two people on earth. Sitting in silence across from one another on silk cushions around a low table, we patiently waited for a sign of life.

After fifteen minutes of sitting in stillness and listening to the rain thump against the dry earth, Su Nim stood up and disappeared into the kitchen. Minutes later, he emerged, a tray in his hands, and glided toward our table, looking regal in his long gray robe. He carefully lowered the tray, which held a large vessel of steaming hot water, an earthenware teapot, a bowl, and two tiny teacups. After a pause, Su Nim methodically poured the hot water into the teapot and allowed the tea to steep for several minutes before pouring it into the cooling-bowl. Then, he clasped his hands together on the table, closed his eyes, and waited for the tea to cool.

I closed my eyes too. In the moments that followed, a deep feeling of peace came over me. Instead of feeling uncomfortable that we were completely alone, I felt at home. In those moments of silence, there was nothing more I needed. I was complete.

I heard the sound of water being poured. When my eyes opened, a steaming cup of green tea sat before me. As I cupped the porcelain vessel in my hands, a feeling of warmth expanded throughout my entire body. I watched Su Nim gracefully pour his own cup of tea, and both of us paused before taking the first sip.

On our very first outing, Su Nim taught that there is a certain way to drink tea in Korea. First, you must feel the warmth of the tea in your hands. Then, before taking the first sip, you must witness the color of the tea. Is it a pale yellow or a deep green? Before the second sip, notice the smell. Is it earthy or sweet? Finally, the taste. Is it full bodied or light and fresh? After the third sip, the tea should be gone—the teacup is only big enough to hold three deep sips. After the third sip, you sit in silence and feel the tea within you. You become one with the tea.

While sitting in silence, I took in the image of Su Nim. He sat so peacefully, eyes shut, witnessing the tea within. My gaze fell upon his bald, shiny head; the way his robe folded and creased in just the right spots. He appeared completely content. If anyone could become his tea, Su Nim had.

It was then that the words arose, pushing their way to the front of my mind—although thankfully not to my lips:

That's my husband.

I looked around the room.

Who said that? I wondered. *And more importantly, did anyone* hear *it?!*

But no, we were still the only two people in the room. The words had, in fact, come from me.

I was confused—I knew that I felt deep love for this monk, but it wasn't a normal, "romantic" kind of love. And those words—*That's my husband*—felt more like a recollection than an actual new idea. It was the same kind of feeling I'd had at the health club in Seattle, when the lifeguard said she was going to Korea.

But this was *inappropriate*! A monk was not a suitable marital partner—a monk was meant to remain alone, and celibate!

I was angry at myself, and conflicted—my heart and my mind at war. My mind was saying, "What are you doing?!" But my heart, the very core of my being, told me that this *was* my husband.

And how do you deny the very depths of yourself?

———————

In May, I found myself taking a weekend trip with Su Nim.

We went to Busan, the coastal city where I had transferred buses on my way to Songgwang Temple. There were plenty of temples in Busan too, and Su Nim had plans to take me to Beomeo Temple to meet some of his monk brothers.

When he first proposed the idea of the trip, I considered telling him I was too busy. I was terrified of what the other monks might think of me for traveling alone with one of their brothers.

But instead of saying no, I simply accepted that I was afraid and hesitant, and I obeyed the stronger voice—the one deep inside telling me that I *must* go; that this was right, despite my worries about how it looked to others.

Su Nim decided it wouldn't really be a visit to Busan without seeing the beach. So instead of going straight to the temple, we had lunch in town and then headed to Haeundae Beach. We found a sunny spot a considerable distance from the shore, away from all the excitement.

Mid-May was markedly warmer than the weather we had earlier in the spring, and the beach was crowded with day-trippers and tourists. We took off our shoes and sat down in the sand. I picked up a handful of the grains and let them sift between my fingers, and felt their warmth between my toes. I lay back on the beach, my black-and-white sundress bunched up around my knees. Closing my eyes, I let the sun beat down on my face.

After a while, I squinted to look at Su Nim. He had chosen to keep his robe on. He must have been boiling with all the layers he had on. He sat with his hands around his knees, staring off into the distance at the kids on the beach digging holes with their shovels, creating deep pools and intricate rivers and filling their buckets with sand to make perfectly molded castles. They were in their own little worlds. The couples sunning themselves on the beach were also in their own worlds, oblivious to anyone else on the shore.

"Do you think the outside world exists, or is it just a creation of our minds?" I asked, breaking the silence.

"What do *you* think?" Su Nim replied.

"Right now I see people on the beach, but I feel like we don't exist to them," I said.

"Why is that?"

"Because they are engaged in their own activities and they're not thinking about us."

"Everything depends on what you think," Su Nim responded. "If you believe you exist in the minds of others, then perhaps you do. But it doesn't really matter what others think of you, does it? It matters what *you* think of you. You create your experience in this world."

I pondered his words for several minutes. I had gauged so much of who I was by what others thought of me that I wasn't quite sure what *I* thought of me.

Who was *I*?

How would I know which thoughts I had collected from others and which thoughts came distinctly from me?

Before I had time to sort out these questions, the conversation had already shifted. We must have talked about everything that day—Buddhism, Karma, connections, travelling, books—until there was nothing left to say. And then we sat in silence and watched the sun go down. When the final speck of sun left the earth, we both closed our eyes and lay still on the beach, listening to the waves until the moon came out.

"Let the moon's energy fill you up; breathe it into yourself, and then breathe it out to the sky." Su Nim said, now sitting cross-legged next to me in the sand. I was so relaxed lying there, but I rose up to a seated position alongside him and followed his instructions. I breathed the moon in, and breathed it out.

Five minutes passed, and then Su Nim continued. "The moon is a powerful meditation tool. It contains everything. You are the moon, and the moon is you. By opening your heart to the full moon, you also become full."

I didn't know how much fuller I could be. I was brimming with the day, the sun, our conversation, the sand, and now the moon. Any more, and I'd be overflowing. I sat there looking at him—his spine erect, legs folded in perfect lotus—taking a deep breath in to let the moon's energy enter and letting out a long exhale to return the moon's energy back to itself. And as I sat there watching him, with the light of the moon on his face and the stars starting to appear above us, I felt the deepest sense of peace I'd ever known.

After a time, Su Nim said, "Do you hear that? Isn't it nice?"

It was guitar music coming from a local café that summoned us to finally leave the beach that night. The single strumming of a one-man show had us walking, mesmerized, in the direction of the sound. We walked toward the bright neon lights of a strip of bars and cafés that fronted the beach. When we found the place, Su Nim looked up at the café's sign, and a smile spread across his face.

"*Mu-ah,*" he read.

"What does it mean?" I asked.

"No self," Su Nim replied. "This is the No-Self Café."

It described exactly how I felt: free of identity, free of self.

I no longer felt the separation between us. "Monk" and "English teacher"—they were just words that created identities, identities we all so desperately cling to. But if we were not "monk" and "English teacher," who were we? Now was a Zen koan to solve, but not tonight.

All the booths and tables were full, so we made our way to the front of the café and hoisted ourselves up onto a couple of barstools in front of a big picture window. The guitarist played with his eyes closed, his right foot gently tapping out the beat of a slow Korean ballad. I did not know the song, but I felt like I understood every word he was saying. It was as if he were speaking to me, telling me, *Open your heart.* I was aware that Su Nim was also absorbed in the music. But eventually the waitress appeared to take our order, bringing us back to the fact that we were customers in this crowded bar.

"*Nok cha i inbun chuseyo,*" Su Nim said. Two hot green teas. Everyone around us was drinking beer and fruity concoctions, but tea had become our custom.

Lost in the music, a warm cup in my hands, a guitarist pouring his soul out through his fingers, and a robed man with a peaceful face sitting silently next to me . . . there was nothing more I needed.

But when the set ended, I was jolted back to reality.

What time is it? I wondered. It had to be after midnight. The temple in the mountains was obviously no longer an option for refuge at this hour. *What is the plan? Where will we sleep?* I was no longer just a figment of my imagination, a "no self." My self was back, in full flesh and filled with doubt and fear.

"It's late. We need to find a place to sleep," Su Nim stated, voicing as fact what I was feeling as fear. Given that it was so late, there was only one option: a *yeogwan* (inn).

As we headed to a strip of *yeogwan* near the beach, my sense of uneasiness grew. I didn't want to go to the reception counter with Su Nim. What would they think about a monk and an American woman getting a room together? But instead of resisting, I followed Su Nim's lead. I'm sure he also felt uneasy, but our options were limited. So was our money. We had not planned to stay in a *yeogwan*, so we barely had enough between us for a room.

I stopped. "How are we going to do this?"

"I'll get the room. You meet me on the second floor," he replied.

Su Nim met me at the top of the stairs and motioned me to follow him down the hallway. I hesitated, scanning for witnesses before continuing. He saw my apprehension and smiled, as if to say, "It will be okay."

Once inside our room, I immediately sat down on the floor. I was a bit shaky. "I'm so glad nobody saw us."

"It's fine," he said. "I think you must feel uncomfortable. I also feel that way."

"I'm okay now that we are inside the room," I assured.

"Yes, we are here now. We have a place to sleep, and that's a good thing. I'm going to wash my face and brush my teeth now."

Su Nim pulled a small towel and toothbrush from his bag and disappeared into the bathroom. I examined the room. It was empty except for two *yo* (sleeping mats) and a couple of comforters rolled up in the corner.

What have I gotten myself into? I thought.

Su Nim came out, and it was my turn to use the bathroom. I went in, sat down on the toilet seat, and stared at myself in the mirror across from me. *What am I doing here?* I worried. *Trust your heart*, said another voice, calm and soothing. I stood up, quickly brushed my teeth, washed my face, and came out of the bathroom. Su Nim was on the floor, in lotus, lighting a stick of incense. He had the two *yo* laid out, side-by-side, blankets on top.

"Let's meditate for awhile," he said. I took a cushion and sat down next to him. I closed my eyes, felt my breath, and let all the thoughts in my mind drop away. I surrendered to the moment and finally just let myself be.

In that silence, I realized how much I truly wanted to be with Su Nim. I felt a deep peace when we were together, but I also felt something magnetic between us—an attraction I always knew was there but was afraid to explore. Ten minutes must have passed before Su Nim got up to turn out the lights. I climbed into my bed and pulled the covers up around my chin. Su Nim did the same. We lay there quietly, trying to fall asleep, but the atmosphere was charged with the energy between us.

Suddenly, I felt Su Nim's hand on my arm, and my heart jumped.

And then I let go again.

My mind had been at war with my heart for so long, and I was finally tired of it. I gave into my heart. I surrendered. The moonlight poured through the window and lit up our faces. Su Nim's embrace filled me with a warm and soothing feeling from head to toe. I let myself be in this warmth. I melted into it.

In those moments of our coming together, the space that separated who I was and who he was simply did not exist. Truly, there wasn't a self to be found. No distinctions, no boundaries, no separations, no black, no white, no right, no wrong. We were the pulse of the universe. We were one.

We never formally talked about what happened between us that night. We knew we had crossed the line in more ways than one. We were no longer tea buddies. We had made love.

But almost as soon as those blissful moments were over, I started to dissect the evening—each piece of it requiring a thorough investigation, like evidence at a crime scene.

And then I'd tear myself up for doing so: *Why can't you just let it be? I* defended. *This is the first time in your life that something feels completely right. Those feelings are so rare,* I argued. *People search their entire lives to find this! Do you really want to turn your back on this just because of what other people might think? Has submitting to outside pressures ever helped you before?*

This was a convincing argument. I knew it was true. I had never gotten anywhere by following what I or other people thought I *should* do and be.

I let these two sides battle it out, and then I fell asleep. In the early morning, just before the sun made its appearance through our *yeogwan* window, Su Nim reached out and pulled me in close to his chest and wrapped his arms around me. I let myself rest in his loving embrace. I felt happy and peaceful. And then it occurred to me: The voice inside me, the one I was trying so desperately to hear, didn't come from my head or by way of my thoughts. It came when I was quiet and still; it came when I let go of trying to find answers; it came when I was in the moment. That voice came directly from my heart.

And in that moment, lying there in Su Nim's arms, I made a pledge to follow it—even though I knew it would not be easy.

In June, Su Nim asked me to accompany him to Songgwang Temple to meet his master. It was sort of like meeting the parents: When Su Nim became a monk, the temple became his family.

The idea of it made me feel awkward. I mean, were other monks bringing women they hung out with (or even slept with) to their masters? Would I be chased by the temple sweepers—the ones I imagined were responsible for keeping the evil spirits out? I didn't want to taint the place. I'd done enough already.

"I'm afraid to meet your master," I admitted. "What will he think of me?"

"Don't worry," he said. "My master will be happy to meet you. You are welcome there."

I replayed those words, "You are welcome," in my head. They were the words I had so hoped to hear when I first arrived at Songgwang Temple the October before. But I'd left without exchanging a word with anyone.

It was a sunny afternoon in June when I first entered the quarters of Su Nim's master. I was nervous as I passed through the rice-paper doors. I was afraid I'd be met by a stern disciplinarian who would scold me for corrupting one of his prized monks. Instead, I was met by the Happy Buddha. A smiling, round-bellied monk with sparkling eyes who was seated in full lotus greeted me as I entered. But his blissful and serene countenance did little to stop me from trembling as I bowed three times to greet him, per Su Nim's earlier instructions.

In the middle of my prostrations, he chuckled a little, as if to let me know that it really wasn't necessary, and then said, "Sit. Sit. Would you like a tomato?"

"Uh . . . sure," I replied, dumbfounded.

No scolding, no lectures, no stern Zen master with a very large stick. Nope. Just a jolly fellow with a great, big tomato.

What's the custom here? I wondered. I hadn't had any discourse on the etiquette of temple tomato eating. *I mean, am I supposed to eat it as one does an apple?* I sat in nervous anticipation of the tomato hand-off as Su Nim and his master discussed life, school, and me—all in Korean, leaving me to interpret what I could on my own.

But during their entire conversation, the tomato sat equidistant from me and the master. It was all I could focus on. Finally, my suspense was relieved as he pulled a grater and a porcelain bowl from a nearby shelf. I felt a mix of awe and surprise as I watched him grate the large red tomato into a fine pulp. He added a bit of honey before passing it to me with an affectionate smile.

I slurped it down. Never mind etiquette. That was that.

Could things be so simple?

Upon devouring the tomato, Su Nim's master smiled in delight. Su Nim later assured me that they hadn't discussed our relationship, but I sensed his master already knew. I could see it in the look in his eyes. It wasn't a look of anger, thank goodness. Instead I felt deep, compassionate love flowing from this man.

After our meeting with the master, we bowed one more time and bid him farewell. Su Nim slid open the paper door, and we descended onto the temple grounds. No one was in sight. Su Nim pointed me in the direction of a path lined with towering bamboo on both sides, creating a kind of private canopy. Once on the path, he grabbed my hand and gave me a kiss.

"Stop!" I commanded through a whisper, so as not to alert the other temple dwellers. I was sure one of the monks would find us there like that and would have evidence enough to usher me off the grounds.

"It's okay, nobody is here," Su Nim assured.

The first time I'd wandered these paths, it was because I'd had an inkling—a premonition, if you will—that I was meant to travel to Songgwang Temple, and that I would meet a very important person there. Truth be told, I'd imagined a great Zen master appearing in a cloud by the river, like a genie, like a bellowing Wizard of Oz, revealing to me my path in life and demanding I follow his advice—the advice I'd been so hungry for.

As it turned out, my Wizard of Oz was a little man behind a long gray robe. As it turned out, my guide was a young monk who was happy to be holding my hand and kissing me.

The sun was high, and butterflies and bees buzzed around us in the early summer air. The bamboo waved to and fro in the breeze, whispering to me, reminding me that these were sacred grounds, that I should respect them. But my temple guide was leading me to believe that all was fine as it was. I was uneasy, but I continued to go with the flow.

At the end of the bamboo path, there was a raised teahouse,

almost like a tree house without the tree. We had to climb a ladder to get inside. Once through the door, I noticed one of Su Nim's brothers sitting at a low table, on a cushion, in silence. He smiled as we entered and motioned for us to sit down. We found some cushions in the corner, arranged them around the table, and joined him. I thought we would at least exchange a greeting, or that there would be some kind of introduction, but we just sat there in complete silence for what felt like time unending.

Not knowing what to do, I closed my eyes and pretended to meditate. Soon, I heard a percolating sound, like a coffeemaker. I opened my eyes to find that it was an electric kettle heating up water in the corner. We were going to have tea.

The monk carefully arranged the teacups on the low wooden table. He set out the tea-cooling bowl, then carefully scooped the leaves out from a canister and placed them into the teapot. He poured the water over the tea and let it sit. After another silent eternity, he poured the tea into the bowl, then crossed his legs and closed his eyes to wait for the tea to cool.

I couldn't help but stare at him and at Su Nim. Here they were, brothers who hadn't seen each other in over a year, and they didn't exchange one single word. I worried that I was the cause of their silence. Or maybe this was this monk's way of treating his guests with reverence. Maybe this was his way of honoring our presence fully. Were words really necessary? Was it possible to honor a guest without exchanging a word?

I tried to imagine having guests over to my house in the States and not saying *anything* to them. I pictured opening the door and motioning them to sit down while I went to the kitchen to prepare a snack and some beverages. No. I don't think this would work. My guests would be uncomfortable, would say, "Is this a bad time?" or "Did something happen? We could come at another time." The silence would throw them off. And what a pity. I can't count the number of times I've been at jaw-dropping places in my life—in the mountains, at a picturesque restaurant, watching a sunset, on a boat heading to one of the San Juan Islands—where words got in the way of fully feeling and enjoying where I was.

The monk reached over to pour the tea into the cups situated at the edge of the table. I watched the light brown color of the tea fill the delicate porcelain cups and waited for Su Nim to take his first sip. He gazed into his cup, noticing the color, then inhaled a long, slow breath, taking in the aroma. Finally, he took a sip, holding the tea on his tongue to fully appreciate its flavor. The monk and I followed suit.

What words were needed? We had the sound of the bamboo swishing in the wind, the high-pitched song of the cicada in the distance. Every single sight, sound, and touch completely filled me. There was more wisdom in this silent encounter than any words of advice could ever impart.

By July, I had almost completed my one-year teaching gig at the language institute. For more than five months, Su Nim and I had been inseparable. We met at school, before school, after school, on weekends. Any chance we could get. Teahouses had become our second homes. Temples too. But I still had my apprehensions about displaying any kind of affection toward Su Nim in public, and I'm sure he did too.

In order to be alone, I would sneak him into my room, or we'd meet at the train station, where he'd change from robes to trekking gear—like Superman in a phone booth—and away we'd go on a weekend trip.

I know that Becky and my other friends had their suspicions about our relationship, but they never asked for details. They knew we spent a great deal of time together, but left it at that. And, being that we were all friends, Su Nim would often join our afterwork group—which consisted of both English teachers and Korean students—for dinner. While we were all out together, Su Nim and I tried not to show any signs that anything was going on between us. The fact that we had to hide our love was starting to wear on me, but it was too soon for Su Nim to know if he wanted to throw everything he knew away for this relationship.

Heck, it was too soon for *me* to know that too.

With my teaching gig ending, I was at a crossroads. I wanted to travel to Japan to meet a Japanese high school friend. He'd called the institute several times, inviting me to visit him at his parents' house. How could I pass up an opportunity like that?

One day, in a little teahouse called Son Lok Wan, in downtown Gyeongju, I told Su Nim of my plans to visit my friend for two weeks. I could feel his heart sink. Two weeks? What would he do without me for two weeks? We hadn't been separated for more than a day or so in five months. I assured him that I'd be back, and that we'd enjoy plenty of time together once I returned.

But the truth was, I didn't know how much time we would have together when I returned. I planned to return to Seattle and then travel some more.

It was hard to speak about leaving, so we wrote about our feelings on the back of a postcard I had in my school bag. The postcard had a picture of daybreak over Toham Mountain, home to several Buddhist shrines. It's thought that the mountain protects the city of Gyeongju. On the back of the postcard—dated Wednesday, July 23, 1996—were these words:

> *Now it's 2:50 PM. We are in the Son Lok Wan teahouse. The music is playing the sound of birds. Very beautiful on this Wednesday afternoon in Gyeongju. I have to leave Gyeongju soon. Tell me how I can be with you.*

I made a row of daisies on the card to separate the space where I wrote and where I wanted Su Nim to write.

> *Now I'm drinking tea. Maybe it's most delicious tea because you are sitting in front of me. Anyway, I'm a little bit sad. Soon you are leaving. I don't know how I can live after you leave. I feel my words are so limited to express my mind for you. But we*

are always together because we have the same spiritual energy.
Please stay with me today.

Was I going to disappear from his life and forget about him?

I really didn't know the answer to that. I still didn't fully understand myself. I wasn't sure I was strong enough to handle this relationship. It seemed it would be easier to let go and lead a regular life with a regular guy. I can't deny it; these thoughts crossed my mind.

He decided to take me to the airport. A crowd of Koreans gawked at us as he embraced me, in full monk robes, in the departure line. I wanted to say something, but the words were stuck in my throat. I was trying hard not to let the tears come out. He stared at me with a look of sadness.

Finally he left me with, "I will see you soon."

I could not watch him leave. I moved forward in line, holding on tightly to all my emotions. My heart was pounding. But going to Japan, I believed, would help. It was a way for me to get some space from Su Nim and to really think about what I was doing. About whether I should continue with this relationship.

The entire time I was in Japan, I was having trouble enjoying all the beautiful experiences on offer. My friend took me to holy sites of the Buddha, Shinto shrines, traditional bathhouses, and delicious sushi restaurants. We went shopping in downtown Tokyo and even watched a Kabuki performance in the Ginza district—but all I could think about was Su Nim. I could have been on top of Mount Fuji—or on the moon for that matter—and my mind still would have been somewhere else.

I tried to be in the moment, but I had definitely fallen into something that most monks train their whole lives to avoid: I had become attached. Perhaps Su Nim had too.

We'd agreed that once I returned, I was to find him at the teahouse he lived above. I'd promised to go there as soon as I arrived in Gyeongju. I had also planned to meet my former students and a few friends there for a cup of tea. My friends all greeted me when I arrived, and I shared stories of my trip over several rounds of green tea. After about an hour, out of the corner of my eye, I saw Su Nim enter. I could tell he did not want to join the circle of friends at the table. He was hoping to meet with me alone.

We rounded up our tea-drinking and conversation and made plans to meet again soon. I walked my friends out but told them that I was going to stay on, that I was planning to meet someone else. No doubt they knew who that was.

As I ascended the stairs back to the teahouse, Su Nim met me halfway. We stood in silence for a minute, and then, seeing that no one was in sight, he pulled me in close. I don't know how long we stood together like that. The thought that someone might see us didn't enter my mind, as it had on so many other occasions. I knew this was right, and I was going to relish this embrace for as long as it lasted.

The next thing I knew, Su Nim was holding my hand and leading me up to the temple portion of the building where he lived. I felt hesitant to enter. I had never been inside before. Were other monks living there?

We sat down on benches near the shoe-storage area, and he held my hand tightly in silence, taking deep breaths. We must have sat like that for twenty minutes, our eyes closed.

It was then that I knew that this was not going to be a short-lived relationship.

Whatever it was that led us to each other, it was beyond our understanding. It was something deep and unexplainable. His hand in mine felt like an extension of myself, like a lost link found again. For how many lives had we been linked, and what form did we take in those lives? Was I his mother? Was he my brother? I had no idea.

What I did know for sure was this: The words "I love you" did not even need to be spoken.

The Treasure Is in Each Moment of the Journey

"Your life is the journey."
—SEONG YOON LEE

TOWARD THE END of our teaching contracts, Mike, Karen, and I started talking seriously about traveling together through Asia for three months—covering Thailand, Nepal, Tibet, and India.

I was excited by the idea, but I worried what I would do about Su Nim. It was hard enough when I went to Japan, and I was only away from him for two weeks. I stopped short of asking him to join us, sure that the temple would not go for this idea. Plus, I was worried about how he would feel traveling with a group of foreigners, particularly with one who was practically his girlfriend.

So imagine my surprise when he invited himself along. Since he planned to visit Buddhist pilgrimage sites while traveling, the temple even agreed to finance the trip, allotting him the cost of airfare and a very modest stipend. My friends knew Su Nim and had spent time with him in group settings, so it didn't seem so awkward for him to join us. Of course, by now they were also aware of our relationship, but they decided to leave that between Su Nim and me. They knew we were a couple and they let us be one without hassling us with questions. This was a big relief.

Before setting off on our journey in August, I decided to go home to visit family and friends for a few weeks in Washington. Then I'd meet up with the others in Bangkok, our first destination. While in the States, I would also take the opportunity to shop for travel gear.

And there was plenty to stock up on. Mike was an avid hiker, skier, and rock climber, and as a result, he was something of a gadget freak. Weeks before I left for Washington, he gave us all a series of lectures on gear—which headlight was the best value; which sleeping bag was lightest and warmest; which hiking poles would be most appropriate for a trek across Annapurna; and whether or not a water purifier was needed.

Before I left, Su Nim wanted to show Mike the sleeping bag he had purchased to see if it was up to Mike's standards. So we went to the temple where Su Nim lived. While we were engrossed in yet another gear discussion, a tiny old monk ran over to the sleeping bag, jumped in, zipped it up around his head, and started wriggling around inside, laughing. Whatever Mike might have thought of Su Nim's new purchase, this old monk was certainly impressed with it.

Frankly, all this gear analysis seemed ridiculous to me. As far as I was concerned, a headlight was a headlight, and a sleeping bag was a sleeping bag. And did I *really* need hiking poles? Or a water purifier for that matter? Were we planning on climbing Mount Everest? Or trekking through giardia-infested rice paddies?

But I'd never been on a trip like this before, so I sucked it up, listened, and took notes. Sort of.

———————

Before I knew it, I was standing in front of Mike and Su Nim at the Bangkok airport, clad in trekking pants, new leather hikers, and a T-shirt, with a bandana around my neck to absorb sweat. At my feet was a Lowe Alpine backpack stuffed with enough gear to make Sir Edmond Hillary blush.

"Hi, Kathy, how was your flight?" Mike asked, giving me a big hug. Su Nim, who stood a few steps back, seemed to be contemplating what sort of greeting to give me. (Clearly, we still weren't completely comfortable showing affection for each other in front of our friends.) He settled on a little wave to me from behind Mike.

"We're all staying on Khao San Road; the hotels are all about the same there; I think we got a pretty good deal," Mike relayed as he guided Su Nim and me out of the airport into chaos. I walked close to Mike, trying to follow the conversation, while Su Nim lagged a short distance behind, my heavy pack slung across his shoulder.

After a long, traffic-jammed, polluted ride, it was late at night when we arrived at the hotel. Su Nim had reserved a room for the two of us. Mike said good night and headed to his and Karen's room. With my backpack still slung over his shoulder, Su Nim led me down the narrow hallway to our room. I followed close behind him in a daze. Having just come from the Pacific Northwest, I was jetlagged and culture-shocked.

The state of our hotel room didn't help. A loud ceiling fan buzzed overhead, but it might as well have been an ornament—it wasn't doing a bit of good. Two twin beds, a single sheet covering each of them, sat side by side. The bathroom had a broken toilet, and the sink and shower drizzled cold water.

I flopped back on one of the beds, exhausted and sticky with sweat. I felt like I had just been spewed out from an exhaust pipe and straight into this hole-in-the-wall.

"What are we doing here?" I asked, remembering Seattle, with its pristine mountains, trees, and clean air.

"You wanted to come here, remember? To travel with your friends," Su Nim said. I pulled him down to the bed and gave him a soft kiss on the cheek. I may have arrived in hell, but at least he was with me. "It will be okay after we get out of the city," he promised.

He'd asked me to buy him some clothes in Seattle, and so I showed him what I'd brought: a few pairs of Gramicci trekking pants, some Teva sandals, and several T-shirts. He held up one of the shirts. On the back was a picture of three monks meditating, the words PREPARE YOURSELF underneath.

"What's this?" he said.

"It's to remind you that even if you wear these clothes, you are still a monk, technically." He looked at me with a half-grin on his face and stuffed it into his backpack.

As much as I knew Su Nim was still a monk, I was elated to finally be free to travel like a regular couple. I couldn't wait to plant a big kiss on his lips in the middle of the open-air market on Khao San Road, where all the tourists mingled. I also had a hunch that we'd eventually branch away from our friends at some point during the trip, which would give us more freedom to do as we pleased.

The next evening, we were all on an overnight train to Krabi, a beach destination in southern Thailand. The others were chatting about things they hoped to see and do on our trip. I tried to engage, but I was still jetlagged and I was having trouble staying awake. Sensing my exhaustion, Su Nim climbed up to the upper bunk, and I lay down in the lower one and closed the curtain tight around me, listening to the rhythm of the train moving over the tracks. I stared up at the top bunk and felt so much gratitude Su Nim was with me. I don't think I could have fully enjoyed the trip with just my friends— I would have missed him too much. Our personal time in Korea had been limited to teahouses, restaurants, day trips around Gyeongju, and the rare weekend trip outside the city, where he sometimes chose to dress in regular garb in order to be my boyfriend. When he was in robes, we had to keep our distance from each other.

Romantic time together occurred on secret weekend getaways, or on the occasions when I managed to sneak him past the guard at the love hotel. Now, here we were in Thailand, finally able to travel as anonymous tourists. In Korea, our roles defined who we were and forbade us from being together, but while traveling, we could be anyone we wanted to be. We didn't need to follow specific rules. No one knew us except our friends. We were anonymous. And there's great freedom in being anonymous. No one expects anything from you. You can be exactly who you want to be. You can be exactly as you are.

Instead of two people with identities, job titles, families, and nationalities, we were just two humans. Two humans stretched out on separate bunks, under starched white sheets, on a train headed for a beach in Thailand. Two humans under the same sky with the same stars and the same moon that all of us in this world share. Two humans in love.

With that thought, I fell soundly asleep for the first time in two days.

———

We rented two bungalows near Railay, a small beach forty minutes from Krabi and reachable only by long-tail boat. We spent more than two weeks there, and the pace was slow. There was nothing to do but swim, snorkel, hang out in a hammock, eat, watch the sunset, and dance to Bob Marley at the bar.

I wanted to pretend we lived there; that our bungalow was our house. That it was a test for Su Nim and me to see how we'd do living together.

Of course, this wasn't real life. I'm not sure how many people hang out in hammocks all day long in real life, or toss a Frisbee around from dusk to dawn. We couldn't always be swimming through crystal blue waters while holding hands, chasing each other up and down white-powder beaches. We wouldn't always be able to watch the sunset every night on a nearly deserted beach. Life wasn't *The Blue Lagoon*. This was just vacation.

But it was heaven.

Still, every now and then, my mind would start to reel, and I would get a guilty feeling, as if we were running from the law. Like we were bank robbers who changed our names, disguised ourselves, and disappeared to an exotic locale with the intention of never being found . . . until of course the FBI shows up on an otherwise perfect afternoon.

And I was feeling dread about our beautiful time coming to an end. Now that we were here in Thailand, traveling like a married couple, I wondered how we could ever continue in this vein. When our love was new, I went with the flow. But now I wanted to know how all of this fit into the bigger picture of life.

"What's going to happen to us?" I asked Su Nim while sitting on the beach one afternoon.

"What do you mean?" he asked.

"I mean, when we return to Korea. How are we going to go out together?"

He was silent.

"I don't think I can take this hiding out anymore," I admitted. "I want to have a regular relationship."

"What can I do about that now?" he said. "Look where we are, Kathy. We are in paradise. We are together. Let's enjoy it!"

Su Nim was right. But still, I couldn't help but feel that it would all come to an end as soon as we returned to Korea. I just couldn't see how it could continue.

"It will be okay. Everything will be all right. We will work it out." Su Nim said, lying on his side in the sand.

I stared up at him through my sunglasses and said, "Are you sure?"

Su Nim did not answer. Instead, he smiled and kissed me, our bodies stuck together from the heat. His soothing words and touch always brought me back to the true moment, and the moments of guilt and fear would pass, like waves dissolving on the shore at sunset.

After two weeks in Thailand, we made our way to Nepal. It was early September now, and we were happy to be in cooler weather. Close to the Himalayas, it really felt like fall there. Becky met up with us, and we all stayed in the Kathmandu Guest House, our base for two months, from which we ventured off on various trekking and traveling adventures.

A journey to Tibet would be our first adventure from our base in Nepal. Tours to Tibet were expensive due to Chinese control over the country, so we decided to make the trip overland by ourselves. The problem was, not many people ventured on their own from

Nepal to Tibet. So there weren't any clear instructions on how to do it. But we had a map, a guidebook, and a general idea of the direction, so with Mike as our designated leader, the five of us set out from Kathmandu on an eight-day overland journey to Lhasa, Tibet. The 924-kilometer stretch of road between Kathmandu and Lhasa—known as the Friendship Highway—turned out to be pretty unfriendly at that time of year: Rain and mudslides had left it in poor condition.

Our first mode of transport was a rickety old bus with folding chairs in lieu of proper bus seats. We were the only foreigners on the bus; everyone else was a local. Given the condition of the road, you can imagine all the sliding around we did on that six-hour trip to the town of Barabise. Once there, we did our best to find a hotel. A trading town for Nepal and Tibet, Barabise isn't exactly tourist-friendly. Finding a place to sleep proved to be more of a feat than we had imagined. After wandering up and down the street on our search, we finally stumbled upon a boarded-up hotel that looked like it hadn't been used in years. A ruffled Nepalese man who was missing a few front teeth decided to open it for us. Thank god for that. We feared we might have to sleep on the side of the pot-holed road. And while we now had a place to sleep in Barabise, there was nothing to actually see there. We had arrived in nowhere land.

The toothless man took out an ancient set of keys and opened the door to the hotel. It creaked as it opened, displaying cobwebs and spiders in every corner. Tired and hungry, we plopped our-selves down at a round table. A puff of dust flew up from each of our chairs—the same dust that covered the table. Mike asked for a menu. *This ought to be interesting*, I thought.

"Wow, they seem to have a lot of things on the menu," Mike observed.

It was true: Listed on the menu were rice, dhal, *momos* (dumplings), vegetable dishes, drinks . . . the works! Things were looking up. Mike ordered a plethora of food from the old host, who didn't have a pencil, pen, or notepad to save him. The man just stood there, looking at us as if we had arrived from Mars. Then he made a single motion with his hand that clearly indicated none of that was available. He picked up the menu Mike was holding and pointed to pancakes and beer. Luckily, we'd brought water, a few cans of tuna, and some crackers to supplement our fare.

We were a little leery about eating the pancakes. *How old is the flour?* I wondered. And it didn't help that there was a very large cockroach in the jam he'd brought out. But we had a place to stay, and we were grateful for that . . . even though we hadn't checked the room out yet.

Oh god, the room. I'm sure large rats must have been in there. The mattresses were thin layers of foam, and the dust from the blankets—which I assumed hadn't been washed in years—was enough to cause a first-time asthma attack.

But what choice did we have? We took it.

The days that followed were a combination of hitching rides and walking over landslides. Finally we got to a point where transportation simply ceased to exist. We ended up walking two hours on a muddy road with spectacular, lush, green mountains shooting up on both sides of us. The road eventually led to the Nepalese town of Kodari, near the border. From there, in order to get into Tibet, we'd have to cross over the roaring Bhote Kosi River via the inappropriately named Friendship Bridge.

I felt like a character in *Romancing the Stone* or a participant on *Survivor*. I mean, was this road—with all its landslides—really going to get us all the way to Tibet? Would the Chinese who patrolled the border even let us cross? And even if we were allowed to cross, how would we get to Lhasa?

I had no idea. I was just happy we had made it this far.

The Chinese border-patrol officer greeted us with a face so cold I'm surprised we didn't instantly freeze into human ice sculptures. I prepared myself for the long walk back over the landslides to Kathmandu, but after listlessly thumbing through our passports, he gave us a wave like he was swatting away a menacing fly. We took it as indication that we were free to cross and scurried over the border without a glance behind us, for fear he might change his mind.

Zhangmu, the Tibetan border town, turned out to be a little paradise compared to Barabise. Su Nim and I were able to get our own room for a change, and actually get that "couple" time we had forgotten about while traversing landslides and picking out cockroaches from jars of jam. We decided to splurge and go out for Chinese food one night. Now that we were in Chinese-occupied Tibet, there was plenty of Chinese food to be had. The restaurant we landed at that night came equipped with our own personal lazy Susan and served everything listed on the menu. We were in heaven.

The only way to travel through Tibet, we learned, was by Land Cruiser. We ended up hitching a ride with two Tibetan filmmakers who were on their way back to Lhasa after filming a documentary about the holy Mount Kailash, where they said they'd spent some time with Richard Gere. Their English was broken, so communication was difficult, but they seemed like our best bet for transportation. So the seven of us stuffed ourselves into a Land Cruiser and headed out on the Friendship Highway, a single-lane dirt road with a drop-off so severe, I was sure it would be the end of us.

The extreme increase in elevation left us all weak. Two of us had to ride in the back of the Land Cruiser, where there was no seats, so we took turns sitting there. Becky lasted the shortest time in the back. She felt nauseated staring over the cliff while bumping along one of the narrowest roads I've ever been on.

After driving for about thirty kilometers, I was happy when our driver decided to make a stop-off at Milarepa's Cave, just outside of the town of Nyalam. I'd been reading a book about Milarepa, the eleventh-century yogi and mystic, ever since I first arrived in Kathmandu, so I was excited to visit the place where he had meditated and shared his teachings for so many years.

I was fascinated by his life story. After his father died and his aunt and uncle ran off with all the family money—leaving his family to live in poverty—Milarepa went to study sorcery. It is said that he caused a storm so powerful that it destroyed the entire village where he lived. Realizing later that revenge was not the answer, he went to study with Marpa, a famous lama in Tibet. After unbelievably arduous training under this master—which included building three stone edifices and then destroying them—he was said to have achieved full enlightenment. It is claimed that he's the only Tibetan saint to do so in one lifetime. After his hard discipline, he had this to share:

> *This, our life, is the boundary mark whence one may take an upward or downward path. Our present time is a most precious time, wherein each of us must decide, in one way or other, for lasting good or lasting evil.*

The hills above the cave were barren; the altitude was too high for anything to grow. The cave was below the roadside and above the Matsang River. There was a small monastery, called Pelgye Ling, where monks lived and tended to the cave.

The driver parked the Land Cruiser on the side of the road and we all stepped out. Young monks and Tibetan children with dirty faces came running to our car to greet us. It was as if we were the first visitors they had seen in months.

Without hesitation, they held our hands and offered us the only food they had: a small boiled potato. We refused, of course. Su Nim got down on his knees, at the level of the children, and hugged them. He could not stop smiling. It was if he were returning home. The children and the young monks took to him right away.

The monk holding my hand couldn't have been more than eight years old. He smiled at me and guided me into the cave. Candles and incense were lit in honor of Milarepa. The monks smiled and motioned for us to sit down. I found a cushion and sat in silence. A tremendous calm permeated my whole being.

What a gift to have the chance to sit in the place where Milarepa once sat. I felt so fortunate to have made it this far.

We didn't have much time to sit and ponder, though, for soon we were ushered back into the Land Cruiser. We had many miles still to cover on our way to Lhasa, and it was starting to get late.

We hadn't even made it to Shigatse, the town where we planned to stay for a night, when we were engulfed in darkness on our one-lane dirt road. This would have been fine, except the headlights on the Land Cruiser failed to operate shortly after they were turned on. It was hard enough being on a single-lane dirt road in the middle of nowhere, but it was even scarier being on it with no headlights, in the middle of the night, without a soul on the road. Who knew how much further we had to go? It was never really clear. What we did know was that we wouldn't be able to continue without light. I was not up for sleeping with seven people in a Land Cruiser, and the options outside our vehicle looked grim.

Those gadgets we spent months pouring over in magazines before we left on our trip were going to finally prove useful. Within minutes, Mike had pulled his high-powered LED headlamp from his bag, and Su Nim followed suit. Mike turned on his lamp and stretched his right arm out the window, lighting up the path in front of us. Su Nim did the same on the other side. With the light of two headlamps, we were able to make it the last hour on the dark road to Shigatse.

We spent the next day exploring our first real city in Tibet; the places we'd been before were just small villages or towns. At the entrance to the city, there was a row of round gold prayer wheels. I lifted up my right hand and spun them before continuing along a cobblestone road. The elevated, bright, gold temple roofs stood out against the backdrop of barren mountains. Doorways and windows were painted in bright reds, oranges, and yellows. Intricate hand-painted mandalas, with the Buddha centered in the middle, covered many of the walls surrounding the temples. We had driven through nothingness on the Friendship Highway and arrived at this gem, in the middle of nowhere. I was so happy to finally see life, but we couldn't stay long. We still had to make it to Lhasa.

Eight days on a bumpy road heading to what seemed like nowhere, with seven of us cramped in a car, at an altitude that would make even the strongest person sick, with drop-offs that made your heart beat in your throat and faulty headlights to boot: It all proved to be worthwhile when we finally got to Lhasa.

My heart sang with the hustle and bustle of the Tibetan capital. Monks chanted in the streets. People carried prayer wheels like cell phones. Children chased us, and rosy-cheeked Tibetans smiled at us from corners and doorways.

The sun was so high in Lhasa that it seemed to lift us all up to a different level. Maybe it was the altitude, but I felt like I was walking above the earth. The sky was the clearest blue I had ever seen, and with the striking gold contrast of Jokhang Temple, I felt like I had entered heaven.

Inside Jokhang Temple, dozens of young monks sat on raised platforms, rocking back and forth and chanting. Some of them would joke and giggle with each other, until the elder monks glanced over at them with disapproving eyes. We wandered around the monks with the local Tibetans. People lit candles, shook their prayer wheels, and chanted. Candles were the only light available inside, and the waft of incense gave us a heady feeling. Lost in a cloud of incense smoke, we moved to the rhythm of the chanting, which seemed to carry us above and beyond the Himalayas.

I felt myself expand and spread in all directions. After traveling this long road to nowhere, I had become a part of everything. I was a part of the monks, the incense, the candles, the chanting, the blue sky, the gold. Everything melded together. I realized in those moments that nothing can be taken from someone whose spirit is strong. No matter what happened on Tibet's soil, the energy of this place remained. And we were all part of it.

Eight days on a dirt road in the middle of nowhere had finally led us to this wonderful place. After spending several days in Lhasa, we had to make our way back to our base for the next adventure. Getting into Tibet was difficult; getting out was a snap. A two-hour flight over Mount Everest had us safely back in Nepal. It was all like a dream.

Back in Kathmandu, we all needed several days of downtime before preparing for our next journey: a trek around Annapurna, Nepal, starting at the town of Pokhara, some 125 miles from Kathmandu. While the others went shopping or wandered around the city, Su Nim and I spent lazy afternoons reading in the courtyard of our guest house. Sometimes I'd take out my diary and sketch pictures of Su Nim reading. We spent hours cuddling, reading to each other, talking about our dreams or ideas, eating in all the cafés in town, shopping, visiting nearby temples, and just enjoying each other's company. It was nice to finally have our own space.

It was starting to become clear that Su Nim and I were in the process of splitting off from the group. The last few days in Lhasa had been difficult: Traveling in a group of any size starts to wear on a person, no matter who's in that group. I was getting tired of following along with everyone like a sheep, but most of all I missed my private time with Su Nim.

Perhaps by default, since Su Nim and I would frequently wander away from the group, Becky started to spend more time with Mike and Karen. Initially, we had all planned to hike the Annapurna Circuit, an eighteen-day circular route through the Himalayas in Nepal that would take us over Thorung La, one of the highest mountain passes in the world. But in the end, Su Nim and I opted to go it alone. I'm sure the others sensed this would be the case, but I still don't know what they really thought of it because we only saw them a few more times during our three-month journey. Perhaps traveling alone with Su Nim was what we both really needed all along, but we weren't ready to fully admit it during the planning of this journey. Becky would end up meeting her future husband, an American, on a beach in Thailand during that same trip, so I guess the universe had its own reason for our parting of ways.

So, the two of us set out together, hitchhiking to the trailhead from a nearby guest house in Pokhara. Once we were dropped off, however, we realized we might have overpacked. Our packs were so heavy; I didn't think we could make it for eighteen days.

Luckily, early on, the owner of a teahouse (which is what guest houses along the trail were called) encouraged us to take a Sherpa with us. He introduced us to Rama, a shy eighteen-year-old boy who was built like an ox. He needed the money for his family, so we decided to hire him. He carried Su Nim's heavy pack, Su Nim carried my pack, and I carried an extra daypack stuffed with various items to lighten the load.

It was the end of September, and the lush green hills along the trail looked like seated Buddhas. The earlier rains had left the rivers pregnant—in some cases, overflowing—and waterfalls gushed from the sides of hills, covering our faces in a refreshing mist. We crossed flimsy drawbridges that hovered over roaring rivers, barely able to breathe as donkeys and locals carrying supplies somehow managed to pass by. Every now and then, a glimpse of the snow-capped Himalayas would open to us. Barefooted children would chase us down the trail with smiles and laughter. Corn grew high, and apple orchards flourished. It was the end of the rainy season, full of life—which made it all the more troubling to see the landslide warning signs along the trail. The landslides here were severe; they took entire houses and people with them, leaving nothing but a pile of rocks in their wake.

At one point, there was a river crossing that I was too afraid to make. But by the time I realized this, Su Nim was already in the icy-cold water up to his waist, carrying his heavy pack high over his head—which meant he couldn't use his arms to balance himself.

"Come back! I think it's too high to cross," I shouted.

He could not hear me and continued deeper into the river until it was well above his chest. Rama was following behind him. I knew that the soil below the river was soft and hard to walk through. He was struggling to get across. My heart was pumping. I was so afraid I would lose him. He later told me that the cold water made his heart slow down to an almost deadening pace. He felt that if he stopped, he would surely die. So he kept moving. Somehow, he scrambled to the shore and just sat there, exhausted, wringing out his clothes.

"I'm going around," I screamed.

An Israeli hiker—a man who'd been hiking all his life—turned to me and said, "I can't believe they crossed there. That's crazy!" He and I walked an extra half mile to an easy crossing spot. By the time we arrived at the hut where Su Nim and Rama were drying off, it was raining buckets. I was soaked through, dirty, exhausted, and still recovering from my fear of losing Su Nim. So I was a little irritated to find him and Rama all cozy by a fire with a cup of tea, socks drying on sticks, laughing about how they had made it across. I told Su Nim we'd have to take shelter for the night at the next teahouse. I could not go any further.

Fortunately, as we climbed higher and higher, the trail dried out. And as we started to approach the town of Manang, at 4,000 meters, the lush green landscape disappeared, and everything became barren.

We would acclimate in Manang for a couple of days, we decided, and then hike across Thorung La Pass. But the thin air at this high altitude was forcing everyone on the trail to slow down, creating a bottleneck in town—there were barely enough beds available at Manang's only guest house. Somehow, we managed to get our own room.

That evening, while having a meal at the teahouse restaurant, we overheard two girls discussing a silent ten-day Vipassana meditation retreat they planned to attend after returning to Kathmandu. Here we were, up at 4,000 meters, and I was finally hearing about meditation. I had been searching for it on this trip, trying to understand its faint calls, following it through the temples and mountains of our journey, but I couldn't hear it clearly.

"It's ten days. I don't know, that seems like a long time to meditate," said one of the girls.

"I know," said the other. "But I want to try it. I've heard it's hard, but that it's also a life-changing experience."

I stood up, and Su Nim gave me a confused look as I motioned for him to stand too. We walked over to the girls, and I said I'd overheard them, and that I wanted to know more. They invited us to sit.

"It's ten days," said the girl who had been trying to persuade her friend. "The course starts about five days after we get back from the trek. I want to try it." And with that, she slid over the brochure.

On the front, on simple, light-blue paper, it read, VIPASSANA MEDITATION. There was a picture of a wagon wheel, and below that, the words, "In the tradition of Sayagyi U Ba Khin, as taught by S. N. Goenka. Introduction to the Technique and Code of Discipline for Meditation Courses."

It was very generic-looking. No bells and whistles. No catchy phrases or color photography showing blissed-out meditators or long-bearded gurus with rosaries. I opened the brochure and saw "Introduction to the Technique." It sounded so technical, like a textbook. But I read on.

> *Vipassana means seeing things as they really are. It is the process of self purification through self observation.*

As I read further, I learned that each meditator would start by observing the natural breath in order to concentrate the mind. From the awareness of natural breath, one would begin to practice Vipassana by observing the changing nature of body and mind. The goal of this path was not just for concentration of the mind. The goal of the path, according to the brochure, was total liberation and enlightenment.

Wow, they're not fooling around, I thought. I'd imagined a meditation course would be more like visiting a spa: I'd go on nature walks, eat excellent food, attend a few lectures, have free time to write and make art.

Nope. Not at this place. The rules called for no speaking, no reading, no writing, no wearing revealing clothing, no communication in way of gestures, no outside communication, no music, no cameras, no tape recorders, no burning incense, no counting rosary beads, no strong-smelling soaps or lotions, no oils, no reciting mantras, no singing, and no dancing.

I read this long list of Don'ts aloud and turned to the girl who gave me the brochure. "What's left?" I joked.

"Meditation," she said with a smile.

I looked at the brochure again. It showed that the registration office was in town, not too far away. But then I saw the course schedule. Apart from short breaks for eating and tending to calls of nature and personal hygiene, the only planned activity, from 4:30 AM to 9:30 PM, was meditation. And then lights out.

"That sounds intense," I said.

"I know," she said. "Just like walking for eighteen days in the Himalayas up and over a five-kilometer-high pass—hard, but so worth it, in more ways than you can imagine."

After a couple nights at Manang, we went to Thorung La Base Camp and stayed the night. The next morning, at four o'clock, we woke up and prepared ourselves for the long trek ahead.

Only groups were allowed to cross the pass, so we hooked up with a Canadian woman and a few English guys. Su Nim and I walked at our own slow pace, but it was reassuring to know that others were a short distance ahead of us. Rama was still with us too.

About an hour into our ascent, the land was so barren, I felt like I was walking on the moon. Nothing could grow at this altitude. The air was getting thinner, and it was difficult to breathe at times.

We had read in our guidebook to be cautious of signs of altitude sickness, as it can hit without warning. You could be a triathlete in perfect health and still be affected. Animals often can't make it over. We saw evidence of this when we stumbled upon a dead horse near the top of the pass. This was certainly no ordinary hike.

As we huffed and puffed to the top of Thorung La, I thought Su Nim might not make it either: About a mile from the top, he started to turn blue.

"Are you okay? You don't look so good," I said.

"Yes. But it's hard to breathe," he admitted.

"Maybe we should go back."

"No, I'll be all right. Let's keep going. I don't want to turn around. We are almost to the top," he gasped.

"He needs to descend to lower ground," Rama said. "He has altitude sickness."

"No. I really think I'm okay," Su Nim assured us.

I was having trouble believing that he was fine, but I took Su Nim's pack, along with my day pack, and we continued to ascend, one baby step at a time.

After less than twenty minutes atop Thorung La, we started our descent. By that time, Su Nim really did not look good and was having trouble walking. I was scared. I'd almost lost him in the river, and here again, I wondered whether he'd be able to make it. We did the only thing we could do—just kept walking down, keeping an even steady pace, without stopping. We must have walked for a good three hours before we were low enough for Su Nim to get his breathing back; only then did we stop for a water break.

We were in the clear again. But I didn't think I could take another risk on this trek. Fortunately, we had made it past all the rough spots. It was all downhill from here.

———————

Back in the crowded streets of Kathmandu, among the Tiger Balm-sellers and rickshaw drivers, I saw, to my surprise, one of the girls from the trek. She told us her friend was about to board a truck for the meditation course, the one we'd heard about.

As soon as she said it, a feeling of familiarity came over me. It was just like the feeling I had when the lifeguard told me she was moving to Korea; just like the feeling I had when I first knew this monk was going to be my husband.

Su Nim and I looked at each other, and before we knew it, we were running through the crowded streets of Kathmandu back to the guest house to let them know that we would not be needing our room for at least twelve days. We frantically threw a bunch of clothes into smaller packs and asked the hotel to store the rest of our luggage until we returned. Then we raced to the registration office to see if we could somehow catch the truck.

When we arrived, there was a long table with smiling helpers asking for our names.

"We didn't sign up, but we want to attend."

I really don't know how it happened, as these courses were popular, but there was space for us. The truck would be departing soon, but we hadn't eaten anything yet. The driver told us there was food and water across the street, so we zigzagged our way through the maze of bicycle rickshaws and cars to the other side. We wolfed down some dhal and rice, bought some water, and boarded the truck. As we bumped along the potholed road, Su Nim said, "Don't have any expectations."

No expectations. I thought that had already been made quite clear to me. After all, how could I have ever expected to be on a dirt road, in the back of a cattle truck in Nepal, headed to a ten-day meditation course with my boyfriend—a monk disguised as a tourist?

But I hadn't completely learned that lesson yet. I did have expectations.

Wow, ten days of silent meditation is going to be divine, I thought. Despite the austerity described in the brochure, I had this idea that once I closed my eyes and crossed my legs, I'd be in perfect peace. *So the rules are a little strict*, I thought. *Who cares? I'm about to experience ten beautiful days of silence! Besides*, I reasoned, *all I have to do is sit and be quiet. After our treacherous hike through rivers and over mountains, that'll be a breeze!*

But soon after the course started, I learned that the brochure left out a few things (or I had somehow overlooked the fine print). I learned that we ate only twice a day. That we had to sit on a thin pad on a concrete floor for up to twelve hours. That the showers only had ice-cold water, which shot out of a tap in the wall as if designed to hose off livestock. My fantasies of the ecstasy I would be feeling on this path toward enlightenment quickly dissolved.

This wasn't bliss. This was boot camp.

And what a crazy mind I was carrying—"monkey mind," as the Buddhists call it. For ten days, I was everywhere but there.

Men and women were separated from each other, and I longed for Su Nim. I wondered how he was doing, but we couldn't speak. I'd get a glimpse of him in the small room that all the foreigners went to for the evening discourse. I'd hear him laugh at a joke during the dhamma talk, and I so wanted to curl up next to him. But I was meant to be alone on this course. I was there for myself—though I was starting to learn that "myself" was full of a lot of garbage, and that on this course, there was nowhere to hide from what was inside. Anger, pain, lust, lethargy; my emotions ran the gamut.

Finally, the relentless pain in my knees from sitting long hours convinced me that this retreat center was really a torture chamber. But I had no one to blame but myself: I came here of my own free will, and no one at the retreat was forcing me to do anything. I wasn't even asked to sit in a certain position. I could even meditate in my room if I really wanted.

Forget climbing the highest mountain pass in the world. Forget forging a river cold and dangerous enough to threaten the life of anyone crazy enough to enter it. The difficulty I felt traversing my *own* inner mountains and rivers far surpassed those travails. This, hands down, was the hardest thing I'd ever done.

On the last day of the course, my eyes met Su Nim's for the first time in ten days.

"I love you," he announced, smiling and full of light.

"Me too," I replied, eyes filled with tears, trying to feign bliss. And then, "Can we please get out of here?"

Su Nim saw through my fake joy and straight into my pain, and at that moment, he gave me the most compassionate smile. He was my guardian angel on this journey, my guide who was patiently waiting for me to open my eyes and finally see myself.

After the course, we spent a very peaceful time in Kathmandu. Strangely, I felt so light, so at ease. At first I thought it was relief I was feeling—relief that the course was over. But then I realized it was more than that. The retreat, I realized, was like surgery: a process of deep, often painful, probing in order to locate and remove impurities that have been festering inside like malignant tumors.

But this feeling of peace and tranquility wouldn't last for long: We were headed for Varanasi, India.

On the flight over, we met a fellow passenger who owned a guest house in Varanasi, the holiest city in India. He gave us his business card. "You have to pay attention in India; you can't just wander here and there without a thought, like you did in Nepal," he warned. "India is not going to make things easy for you. You have to abide by her ways."

I just smiled and said, "Thanks for letting us know." I didn't give it much more thought . . . until we were on a rickshaw in the middle of a polluted intersection with cars, chickens, camels, cows, beggar women and children, motorcycles, and bicycle rickshaws going every which way. I couldn't even see the street. It was complete chaos. And then my backpack fell off the rickshaw.

"My pack!" I shouted.

But the rickshaw driver kept going. Su Nim tapped him on the shoulder and said, "Stop! Our pack fell off!" With that, Su Nim scrambled off the rickshaw and disappeared into the street. We had just arrived in India, and he was already swallowed whole.

Amazingly, Su Nim was able to retrieve the pack, and the rickshaw dumped us off near a row of guest houses. While standing in the street, an army of children approached us, prepared to carry anything we had. One carried my water bottle, one carried Su Nim's pack, one carried my pack, and the last one carried my jacket. We tried to let them know that we did not need any help, but they were determined.

"Where you want to go?" shouted one of the children.

We handed him the guest-house's card, but that's not where we ended up. They took us to a relative's guest house, and then all of them demanded rupees. We paid each one of them. At this point, we didn't care—as long as we had a place to rest.

But bars lined the window of our room, and there were no blankets on the battered mattress. In the hallway was a squat toilet covered with feces. It was a cement prison cell as far as I was concerned.

Su Nim lit incense, took out our sleeping bags, and blew up a few air pillows. The place was getting better. He had a way of making a dungeon look classy.

We lay there hugging each other, and I just started crying. I was ready to settle somewhere together. I was getting tired of traveling. He brushed the hair from my forehead and said, "It'll be all right. We don't have to stay here." After about an hour I fell asleep to the soft music from his cassette player and the smell of incense.

The next morning, we rose at dawn and wandered down the cobblestone road toward the Ganges River. A twelve-year-old boy ushered us into his rowboat and took us on a sunrise trip up and down the Ganges.

Here we were, at one of the holiest places on earth, and I was horrified. Trash floated by, children defecated up on the ghats along the river, women washed clothes and brushed their teeth in the murky water, and bodies burned nearby. (In India, it is an honor and a blessing to have ones ashes or bones, for those who can't afford a full cremation, thrown into the Ganges.)

Intermingled with these horrors were yogis and sadhus (wandering holy people) reciting the most beautiful chants. People sat in full lotus, meditating with peaceful looks on their faces. Amid the chaos, clarity was present. The river was calm, and the sunrise was breathtaking.

We went on a day trip from Varanasi to Sarnath, the place where the Buddha gave many sermons. I had to close my eyes during the entire trip there: So much was going on in the street, it was too much to take in. By the time we got to Sarnath, I was a basket case, and it took me a good half hour to calm down and enjoy this place of peace.

One of our last stops in India was Agra, the home of the Taj Mahal, and by the time we reached it, I fell completely apart. We had traveled all night to this place after missing our original train—only to be sold tickets on another one with no seats. We slept on the floor with chickens and suitcases, and somehow ended up getting off at the wrong stop. We were stranded in a very seedy-looking train station in the middle of the night. People stared at us as if we were extraterrestrials. We couldn't find anyone who spoke English. Finally, a man said, "You want to go Agra? That train is going, but it will leave now. You better hurry up." We had to run across three tracks to get to the train. How did we know it was really going to Agra? But then again, what was the alternative?

It was completely dark on the train—there were no windows, just bars. It was definitely a third-class train. Someone lit a lighter, and we were able to find one seat, and both of us squeezed into it. The train started moving, and we prayed it was going in the right direction. Su Nim said to the man with the lighter, "Agra?" and he just looked at us blankly. When the first crack of light appeared, the train conductor came by to collect money, and we learned that the next stop was Agra.

With the sun rising over the Taj Mahal, we took a rickshaw to a nearby hotel. I collapsed on the lobby sofa as Su Nim went to check us in. We followed an Indian man up to look at a room, and by the time we had returned to the lobby to get a room key, Su Nim's money belt—which was stuffed into the top of his pack—was gone. I berated him for leaving it behind in the lobby.

"You have to pay attention in India! Don't you remember what the guy on the plane said?"

But it was too late. The entire hotel staff denied any knowledge of the money belt. All of Su Nim's money, all of his traveler's checks, and his plane ticket back to Korea were gone. Thankfully, for some reason, I had Su Nim's passport in my money belt. We were upset but too tired to search for another hotel, so we checked into the room.

I spent the next two days on the toilet.

I'd acquired amoebic dysentery and ended up, in the course of two days, losing over ten pounds. I couldn't hold down anything, not even soup. I encouraged Su Nim to go out and get some fresh air. He decided to meet up with an Englishman for a *lassi*, a delicious yogurt drink. When he came back, he was bouncing off the walls.

"Are you okay?" I asked, still crippled over in pain.

"Yes, but I feel weird," he said.

"Well, what did you have today? Maybe that had something to do with it," I said sarcastically, as someone who was definitely "feeling weird" because of something she ate.

"I had the special *lassi*," he said.

I turned my head and stared at him with raised eyebrows. "Um, that's not a *lassi* with extra fruit, you know."

"What do you mean?" he said.

"Well, I think it means they sprinkle it with hashish."

"With what?" he said, trying to focus.

"Umm . . . it's like marijuana, only stronger."

He put his head in his hands and chuckled. Before I knew it, he had rolled over on his side and was snoring away. I finally managed to get some sleep too, and the next morning, I felt strong enough to venture over to the Taj Mahal.

I wanted to stay there forever. It was an oasis in the middle of all the craziness. We took off our shoes at the entrance and walked barefoot on the cool white marble as a light breeze blew. I sat down, leaned against a wall, closed my eyes, and meditated.

At first, my mind was clouded with doubt. *Do I still know how to do this? Have I already forgotten everything I learned in Nepal? Have I forgotten how to observe? Have I heeded the advice of the man on the airplane? Have I really been aware here in India?*

And then all of that faded. All of that changed. I was here, now, at one of the Seven Wonders of the World. And I was fully present.

I drew in a long, conscious breath through my nose and let it fill my lungs and then breathed it out slowly. I felt the heat and light of the sun enter in me and expand throughout my body. On my exhale, the light moved out and spread in all directions, returning to where it had come from. The smell of incense, the voice of another tongue reciting a mysterious chant from inside the walls of this holy shrine, the pitter-patter of bare feet walking gently past me—all was not separate from myself. Everything was contained in that moment.

Everything *is* contained in *this* moment.

Back in the temple in Korea, where I struggled to understand meditation, it was Su Nim who first brought this truth to my attention. While I knew these words were right, I wasn't always comfortable with the uncertainty of what the moment would bring. I wanted to know what would happen to Su Nim and me. I eagerly wanted to find that elusive pot of gold that would bring me happiness, peace, and bliss.

Now I realized that each moment of this journey—even the ones in which I was consumed by exhaustion, fear, or pain—were important. And during most of those moments, Su Nim was right by my side. I was grateful he was there, but he could not protect me from the emotions and physical discomforts I would feel. We were together, yet separate—each of us experiencing this journey through our own eyes. I knew, after our trip, that I wanted to be with Su Nim, but I also knew I had a lot to work out about myself and my direction in life.

I spent the last moments of my trip alone in the Bangkok airport. Su Nim left on a flight back to Korea, and I was about to head home to Washington for a few months to meet family and friends before returning to South Korea for another teaching gig at the same school. I found a quiet spot in the waiting area and took out my journal and composed this letter to Su Nim dated November 23, 1996:

Dear Su Nim,

Hi, I'm in the Bangkok airport about to head to L.A. and then on to Seattle. I'll be on this plane for a long time. Anyway, I'm okay. How are you? I hope you made it to Korea without any difficulties. I had a really nice trip with you, even though sometimes I was angry or had a bad temper. Maybe the fortune teller/hand reader at the temple was right. Anyway, I'm sorry if I bothered you at times. I know I need to be more equanimous. You, on the other hand, are the epitome of equanimity. I wish I could be more like that too—more easygoing and relaxed. You are a very good travel partner.

I don't know my future. Sometimes I think I should have some big plan for my life, but I know that's not important. And sometimes I think I want to be with you forever, but I don't know my life and I don't know your life. I want an answer from life, but there is no answer. Here and now . . . here and now. Anyway, I hope to see you more in my life. You have changed my life. Your existence is so important to my existence. I know that now.

I love you,
Kathy

I knew that Su Nim was in my life for a reason. Perhaps he was there to show me that life was happening right in front of me and that there was nowhere to get to except where we were. And that was enough . . . for now.

To Be Happy Together, First Learn to Be Happy Alone

Alone means "all one."
—SEONG YOON LEE

B Y FEBRUARY, I was living in Gyeongju again, and Su Nim took up residence in a temple in the next town over.

It was challenging being a couple in Korea again. We had to be strategic about our meetings. We'd hide out in video *bangs*, where people watched movies in order to escape the confines of crowded living quarters. We'd tuck ourselves behind trees in parks. It wasn't an easy situation, and I wasn't sure how much longer I could sneak around with a monk. It tugged at my conscience.

We managed to live like this through the spring and summer, but by fall, Su Nim was gone. He went on another pilgrimage to India with a monk friend, and I was sure it was to forget about me.

I knew he was conflicted—he felt like he had to choose between the temple and me. Monks in the Chogye order, the lineage that Su Nim belonged to, do not marry and are meant to lead celibate lives. Obviously, trying to secretly live these two very different lives was taking its toll on him—and on me.

But how could I expect him to choose? After all, we were both still in our twenties. Sure, we were happy and in love, but making a decision about our entire future seemed a little premature. I, for one, was still trying to sort out my purpose in life. Besides, being a monk was all that Su Nim had known. He didn't have any other job skills. What kind of career does a monk transition into? How do you give up all that you know for something so uncertain?

Even though he had broken the rule of celibacy, Su Nim wasn't ready to hang up his robe. Though his monk brothers might have guessed what was going on, no one was keeping tabs on him or demanding he give up monkhood. That wasn't really how it worked in Buddhism. It was his own conscience that governed his decisions.

———————

Su Nim became a monk when he was only nineteen. While many of his friends were studying to become doctors or lawyers, he had no interest in such pursuits. He was looking for freedom.

Raised by his grandparents after his parents' difficult divorce, all he could think about was how to be free from the conflict and strife relationships appeared to cause. While studying Buddhism in college, he was sure that all the scriptures he read were pointing him in the direction of meditation. On his way back to college after winter vacation his sophomore year, he stopped to visit his uncle. Later that day at the station, about to buy his ticket back to school, his inner voice said, *That is not where you need to go.*

So instead, he bought a ticket to Songgwang Temple. He had no idea what was happening to him. It wasn't something he pondered over; it was as if something or someone was choosing for him.

Su Nim is the kind of person who, once he makes a firm decision, doesn't look back. So much so that he didn't let his family know that he had become a monk. They were accustomed to the fact that he rarely got in touch with them, and so they had no idea he'd traded long hours of studying in the college library for long hours of monk training at a remote temple.

One afternoon, a friend of Su Nim's grandmother was watching the Buddhist Network when she nearly lost her dentures. She shouted *"Aye-go!"* (I'm dying!) at what she saw on the television: There was Su Nim, clad in gray robes, demonstrating step-by-step how to make temple rice. Staring at the screen in disbelief, she called his grandmother.

"Your grandson is making rice on TV!"

Su Nim's grandmother turned on the TV and collapsed into her armchair. There he was, her grandson—who had such a great future, whom she had so many hopes for—carefully washing the white grains and placing them in a pot to boil. Unable to fully believe what she saw, she gathered the entire family together the next day to make a trip to this temple and to see with her own eyes what had seemed like an illusion.

Once at the temple, she made her way around the grounds in a frantic search and was relieved not to find him anywhere. But then, suddenly, she saw Su Nim emerge from a building, his bald head glistening in the sun, and his gray robes flapping behind him.

She fainted on the spot.

It took her years to accept the decision made by her grandson—a boy who had really been a son to her. She died several years later, before I ever had a chance to meet her (no doubt sparing her a second fainting spell).

Su Nim had such a strong feeling about being a monk that he was willing to sacrifice his ties with his family to do it. How does a monk who seems predestined to be in the temple suddenly leave that all behind for a woman? And, as if becoming a monk wasn't hard enough on his family, how would he break the news to them that he now had an American girlfriend? I'm sure all of these questions were too much for him to bear. It was easier to just disappear than to have to make any decisions on this matter.

With Su Nim gone, I decided to go back to Washington and take a break from my life in Asia. I let my school know that I'd return in January. Su Nim promised to write. After three months with no word, a crumpled postcard dated December 12 arrived in my mailbox. It read,

> *Hi, how are you? I'm in Rajgir, in Bihar State. There was a riot and gunshots yesterday, but I'm O.K.*
>
> *Love,*
> *Su Nim*

I imagined him walking down the street, his long robe floating behind him, a bullet coming within centimeters of his ear. He managed to escape Rajgir unscathed, but it was spring before I heard from him again.

Stuck in limbo, with Su Nim lost in India, I had no idea what I should do. I stayed home for six months, three months longer than I had planned. An economic crisis had hit Korea, and the school where I taught no longer existed. With few employment options at home as well, I ended up taking a job at a coffee shop down the road from my parents' house.

It was embarrassing to work there. People I knew from high school and hoped I'd never see again would frequent the café. There I was in an apron, wiping down tables. On one occasion, a woman exclaimed, "Kathy Jenkins? Hi! Is this where you've been since high school?"

I just smiled and said, "Not exactly."

Desperate to get out of my hometown, I found a teaching job in Japan. Going back to Asia to teach English again made sense. After all, I had experience teaching English, and there didn't seem to be a lot for me at home, nor in Korea. I felt torn about leaving Su Nim and Korea, but given the economic climate, Korea was just not an option.

I arrived in Sendai, Japan, on a freezing March day. The owner of the language school, Mrs. Edwards, was the Japanese wife of an American man. She met me at the airport, along with Cindy (the teacher I'd be taking over for) and Ayako (the office assistant).

Mrs. Edwards didn't waste any time. "Hi, how was your trip? We gonna show you around Minami [South] Sendai, take you to the schools, have lunch, you can look the apartment, then you can stay with me 'til Cindy move out, okay?" Before I knew it, we were outside the airport, heading to Mrs. Edwards's van.

The moment we stepped outside, I realized I had underdressed. I instantly felt my face and hands go numb from the cold. Cindy, who was from Canada, sat in the front seat wearing a huge down jacket, gloves, a scarf, a hat—and this was in the *car. Did I pack warm-enough clothes?* I wondered. *And by the way, why isn't the heat in the car on?*

They showed me around the two schools I'd be teaching at. They were well-worn, dated, and small—each classroom only big enough for ten students and me. And the classrooms, like the rest of Sendai, were freezing. Our breath came out in a white fog and my hands were icy cold.

"Is there a heater in here?" I asked, rubbing my hands vigorously together.

"Yes of course," said Ms. Edwards, pointing to a kerosene heater on the floor.

Wait a second, I thought. *Isn't Japan supposed to be high-tech? Am I in the right country? Have I landed in the Dark Ages?*

After lunch, Mrs. Edwards dropped Cindy and me off at the smaller school, and we walked a few blocks to my future apartment—the one that Cindy would be occupying for another week while I stayed with Mrs. Edwards.

This was Cindy's first venture outside her homeland, and I was still trying to get the feel of whether or not she had enjoyed her time here. I suspected, however, that she was pretty homesick—she'd already spent a lot of our time together talking about everything she was going to do when she got home. Once we arrived at the apartment, my suspicions were confirmed: Her suitcases were already sprawled out on the floor, a full week before her departure.

The apartment—housed in a dated metal building—had a sliding door that separated a closet-like bedroom from the even smaller TV/living room, and another sliding door that separated the TV/living room from the kitchen. The bathroom was only big enough for one person but had a deep plastic tub inside. That tub—into which flowed the only source of hot water—would become my refuge.

"There's no hot water in the kitchen?" I asked, a bit surprised, as Cindy continued to show me around the place.

"Nope. Gotta get the hot water from the tub and bring it over to wash the dishes."

The hot water situation wasn't the only problem. I also learned that the only way to survive the winter was to close yourself off in a room with the apartment's ancient kerosene heater—which, when ignited, made a *tick, tick, tick*, followed by a startling *whoo-PAH!* and a cloud of smoke (never mind the risks posed by inhaling toxic fumes at such close proximity).

I was already feeling freaked out by this living scenario. Sure, I had traveled quite a bit and had survived uncomfortable, even scary, situations—but none of which I had to live with in the long term. And none of which involved asphyxiation in my sleep. I actually found myself suddenly pining for my old Korean love hotel and its karaoke women of the night.

"How do you change the gas?" I asked.

"The gas guy comes once a week. You just put your gas canister out on the front porch, and if they see it there, they will fill it. Then you bring it in and stick the gas tube into the hole on top of the kerosene heater and pump it until you see the line move, indicating that it is full."

Seattle, I took you for granted. I'm sorry. Please take me back.

I chatted a bit longer with Cindy about the odds and ends of the job, and finally, I just cut to the chase.

"Did you have a good experience?" I asked.

"I'm looking forward to getting out of here," was her reply.

Great. I'm already looking forward to the same thing, and I just got here!

It started getting dark outside, so Cindy escorted me back to Mrs. Edwards's house, which seemed palatial compared to the hole I'd be staying in. But it too was freezing.

What is it with Japan and the cold? I thought. *Is this some kind of endurance test? Is the country experiencing an energy shortage?* I just didn't get it.

I had a cup of tea with Mrs. Edwards, who only wanted to talk about the school. She was a live wire, all right. Her small frame barely contained all of her energy. She was determined to give me the full scoop in one night.

I imagined Japanese women to be demure and overly polite. But Mrs. Edwards? Not so much. Maybe she'd been Westernized by her American husband, because she skipped the pleasantries and cut right to the chase. Within seconds, I was getting the nitty-gritty details; nothing was spared. I heard all the gossip about the other teachers who came before me. I was sure that stories about me would soon be added to the script.

It wasn't long before I'd had enough. "I think I'm going to read and then go to bed," I said.

She seemed puzzled that I was cutting our one-sided conversation short but led me upstairs to a child's room with an old wooden bed.

"This was my son's room, but my children are all living in America now."

I don't blame them, I thought, shivering and looking at the unlit kerosene heater in the corner. Even in my room, she blabbed on about the plan for tomorrow. But today alone had already been a little overwhelming for me, and I had trouble focusing by this point.

Finally, Mrs. Edwards left, and I crawled under the cold sheets and stared at the ceiling, confused and alone, before falling asleep.

A week later, I moved into Cindy's old apartment. I still had no news from Su Nim, but I'd given all my contact information to my friends in Korea, thinking that might be my only way of letting him know.

Meanwhile, I tried to carry on with life. I halfheartedly listened to explanations about lesson plans and textbooks, tips on where to shop for groceries, and how to get from point A to point B. I went through the motions of starting a new job and a new life in Japan, but my heart wasn't in it. My heart was with Su Nim.

But who knew where his heart was—or even where *he* was, for that matter? What would happen when he came back to Korea to find me gone? I wasn't sure if he was dead or alive, or if I'd ever see him again. I wasn't even sure he *wanted* to see me again. These thoughts cycled through my head as I shopped for groceries, pumped kerosene, washed laundry in the most primitive machine I had ever seen, hauled hot water back and forth from the bathroom, walked to and from the two schools to teach, and mopped and locked up for the night.

I was lonely. I knew no one. Nearly every night during those first few months, I'd lie awake on my futon and ask myself, *What am I doing here? And why am I not with Su Nim?*

As it turns out, I was right: Su Nim *had* gone to India to forget about me. But he was unsuccessful.

Immediately upon his return to Korea in mid-April, he went on a mission to track me down. Desperate to find me, he went straight to the house where I'd lived, only to discover I wasn't there. Fortunately, he managed to get in contact with my friends, who told him I'd gone to Japan and gave him my phone number.

I was closed off in my kerosene-heated room, eating lunch and staring out into nothingness, when he called. I picked up the phone, and there was dead silence. I knew it was him. I couldn't breathe. I swear I could hear his heart beating.

"Kathy?" he finally whispered, almost gasping in disbelief.

"Yes, it's me, Su Nim." Tears started to roll down my cheeks.

"I love you," he said.

More silence.

"I love you too."

He told me he'd bought a ticket to Japan; that he needed to see me right away. He said it had been unbearable being without me, and that he would be in Tokyo tomorrow.

———

Su Nim arrived at Narita airport in Tokyo the next day with not much more than the robe on his back. He had managed to scrape together just enough from friends to get himself to Tokyo, only finding out once he got there that he would not be able to cover the cost of the bullet train to get to where I was. Fortunately, I had a friend who'd met Su Nim once before and who offered to pick him up and let him stay a night at his parents' house near Tokyo. The next day, our friend took Su Nim out to lunch and bought his train ticket to the town I was living in, located two hours north.

Since I was teaching, the school assistant, Ayako, agreed to pick him up.

Ayako was the only person who knew how much pain I had been in without Su Nim. Mrs. Edwards had left for the semester, so Ayako and I ran the two schools together. I'd often be teaching at one school while she taught at another, but we'd meet up for lunch sometimes to debrief each other. Out of sheer loneliness, I'd tell her my woes about Su Nim. She was kind but distant. She would always listen to me, her head nodding as if to say she understood, but it was hard to tell if she really wanted to listen, or if she was just being polite. Yet she went above and beyond the call of duty by agreeing to meet Su Nim at Sendai station and to drive him to my apartment.

By the time they arrived, I had cleaned, loaded my fridge, changed my clothes, fixed my hair, and gone through an imaginary dialogue in my head of what I would say to Su Nim. After all, it had been six months since I had laid eyes on him. I worried I'd forgotten what he looked like, and whether I would remember his touch. I'd tried to imagine the moment we'd meet again many times. I'd played that scenario over and over on the movie screen of my mind, but nothing could have prepared me for the real thing.

I heard the sound of gravel under tires. A car pulled in the drive and parked outside the sliding door of my bedroom. I knew it was Ayako and Su Nim.

Ayako escorted him to the door, and when she saw me open the door, she gave a little wave and smile, then turned and left. Su Nim stepped up onto the ledge and entered through the sliding glass door. I was already sitting on the tatami floor when he came in. Upon seeing him, I started to shake. He fell to the floor and embraced me. As we clung to each other on the floor, the tears came. I couldn't hold them back any longer. They streamed down my face and wouldn't let up. Su Nim looked at me and couldn't hold back either. I had never seen him cry. He cried out loud. He said he had tried to forget about me. He had tried to erase me, but he couldn't. This love that he had tried to extinguish was stronger than he was.

Unfortunately, he could only stay for two weeks—that was all the Japanese government would allow.

But for the next two weeks, we were glued to each other's side, apart only during my classes. And during that time, he decided to lose the robe and to wear regular clothes again. We were back to being tourists in disguise. No one knew us. We were *gaijin* (outsiders), as the Japanese called us.

One afternoon, while riding bikes on the elevated path between two rice fields behind my apartment, we stretched out our arms and held hands while pedaling. We rode that path all the way to the ocean, where we laid our bikes down in the sand. The beach was empty. I grabbed Su Nim's hand, and we ran the entire length of the beach, waves crashing on the shore. Later, tired, we curled up together against a sand wall and stared at the Pacific.

Once again, we were anonymous and alone, stripped of identities, with an endless sea and naked beach before us.

Back in my room that night, we lay down, facing each other on my single futon.

"I don't know what I'm going to do when you have to leave," I confessed.

"I'll be back soon," he promised, and then reached for my hand, giving me a look that told me he meant it.

After that, I didn't think about Su Nim leaving. I lived in the moment. I was happy to be with him, and that changed my attitude about my environment. I started to see beauty all around me. Everything suddenly seemed bright. All my senses were alive again.

Japan really was a wonderful place. The food in the restaurants we frequented was delicious. Downtown—which I rarely went to on my own—was full of life, with all the neon signs and people everywhere. The Shinto shrines, the Buddhist temples and their gardens—they were such peaceful places where we'd often meditate, rest, and read to each other.

When Su Nim was with me, even grocery shopping was exciting. We strolled down the aisles, throwing mysterious Japanese items in our cart—*natto* (fermented soybeans), seaweeds of all kinds, and odd-looking seafood—and then we'd walk arm and arm back to my apartment to prepare a feast fit for the gods. Other nights, we'd hit a few karaoke rooms and go out to dinner. But the best time was the weekend we ventured out of my little neighborhood by JR train and Shinkansen (bullet train) to a sleepy little hot-spring town.

With Su Nim by my side, I wasn't afraid to go anywhere or try anything.

———

Su Nim kept to his word and came back as soon as he could—four months later, in August—for another two-week stay. Two months later, in October, he came again, for another two weeks.

But in the second year, his visits stopped.

Next to the door of my apartment was a mail slot. Every day after Su Nim left in October, I couldn't wait to get back to my apartment to check it. It was what kept me going through the seasons, which came and went at a snail's pace when Su Nim wasn't around. I could almost feel the golden shafts of rice slowly inching their way up toward the blue sky in the fields I rode my bike through every day.

By late November, these grains had been cut down to the nub, leaving the once-beautiful fields now naked, raw, and unchanging, like a wound that would not heal.

By the time December rolled around, the grounds were frozen solid. Riding my bike along this path was no longer pleasant; it chilled me to the bone.

But the letters I received from Su Nim helped me feel like I was not alone during the months, days, hours, and minutes that painstakingly crept by. Su Nim used to say to me that the word "alone" actually means "all one." That it didn't matter where we lived, we all experienced the changing of the seasons. But I had trouble feeling "all one." Every now and then, I'd feel the moment. I'd feel the wind shift on the bike path, or the rain touch my skin, and I'd realize I wasn't the only one feeling these things. But most of the time, after the thrill of a new letter wore off, I felt alone.

After riding my bike home in the midafternoon between classes, I'd always say hello to my neighbor, who spent most of his time in his garden behind my apartment. In the spring, he'd be out picking flowers or pruning bushes. In the summer, I'd find him with a cool tea, sitting on a stump under the shade of a pine tree. Fall was all about raking leaves, and winter was apparently meant for shoveling snow.

"*Konichiwa!*" I'd shout whenever I saw him.

"*Ah, konichiwa!*" he'd reply, raising his head from the task of the day with a smile and a bow.

That's about as far as our conversations ever went. Even though I was studying Japanese, I didn't have the confidence to engage in a full-fledged conversation, nor did I have the desire. I wasn't in Japan to make lasting friendships. I was in Japan to make a living and to learn how to be on my own. At least that's what I believed at the time.

Obviously, I hadn't mastered being on my own at all, because I couldn't wait to see if there was any news from Su Nim. After leaning my bike against the side of the apartment, I'd close my eyes and try to visualize a letter on the concrete floor below the mail slot. Most of the time, there was nothing.

On those days, I'd make myself a cup of tea and sit alone at my dining room table and just stare out the window or blankly in front of me.

On the days the letters would arrive, it was like I had received my food ration for the month. I'd rip open the envelope and devour its contents, and then I'd go back and hang on to every word for seconds at a time. But there were times when months passed with no words, and during those times, I felt like we were breaking apart.

I still hoped and prayed it would work out, but I was starting to let go. Phone calls were few and far between, due to the remote location of the temple where Su Nim now resided, but when he would call, I found it difficult to hold anything back. All of the emotions I'd been holding on to for months would come flooding out like water released from a dam. Often the conversation ended in tears, or was left unresolved, which spurred more conversation of the written variety, like this letter dated April, 27, 1998:

> *Dear Kathy,*
> *After I called to you, I thought a lot. I don't know what I have to do. Kathy loves me. I love Kathy. But I'm a monk. It's like a dilemma. Anyway, I have to make a decision. You said we can't hide each other and we can't live like this. What if I take off monk clothes to become social life, like get a job and make*

a money, etc.? . . . Actually, I'm afraid about that and I'll feel guilty. I don't know. Anyway, I love you so much. I assure I can't meet like you in my life. You're my everything. Also, in my mind, I want to keep my monk life. You want my answer, also I want to know my answer. Still, I have no answer.

And my reply, dated May 6, 1998:

Dear Su Nim,

Hello. How are you? I got your letter today, and I don't want to bother you too much. I am sorry I cried on the telephone. I hope you have a nice meditation. I know I shouldn't send too many letters, but another three months without speaking to you is going to be difficult. When you finish your meditation it will be August. I have only seen you ten days in about one year. This love we have is the most important thing to me. There is no question and no answer about anything in my mind. The only thing that exists in my mind is Su Nim, and I want to be with Su Nim. That is my answer. But I am not the only one. I must think about you. What is important to you?

I didn't sign this letter. I didn't even send it. I kept it in a pile with all the other letters I had received from Su Nim. I don't know if I ended up sending him anything like the letter above. I honestly don't remember. But those were my thoughts. That is how I felt.

I know it was hard for Su Nim to be without me. The hardest

time was the second summer we spent apart from each other. He was in the mountains in Gangwon province, in the northeastern part of South Korea, meditating alone in a hut owned by a rice and vegetable farmer. He went for days without meeting a soul. The farmer's wife would prepare food for him every two weeks, and the farmer, who lived in the valley below, would carry these staples up the mountain for him. After three months of solitary living, Su Nim decided it was time to hike down the mountain and come back to civilization.

The day he arrived at the farmer's house, he got a phone call from one of his monk brothers, informing him that the woman who loved him like a son—his grandmother—had just passed away. He froze with the phone to his ear and managed to croak out *"Agesumnida . . . gamsamnida"* (I understand . . . thank you). When he hung up the phone, he fell to the floor, sobbing loudly.

Seeing him in pain and not knowing how to console him, the farmer's wife got down on her hands and knees and began to peel potatoes. Less than thirty minutes later, she had prepared a potato pancake for Su Nim.

The love that came with this dish instantly soothed him, and he realized that even though he had lost his grandmother, love still remained in the world. Days later, he quietly made his way back to his hometown for the funeral. He missed the cremation ceremony but led the funeral by chanting Buddhist sutras. He had performed many of these ceremonies in his life as a monk, but none had been so heart-wrenching as the funeral for his beloved grandmother.

Shortly after that, his grandfather passed away, perhaps from the heartbreak of losing his lifelong partner. Su Nim was again struck with overwhelming sorrow as he led his grandfather's cremation ceremony. His family members wailed in the background as he chanted and washed his grandfather's dead body with his own hands, trying to keep himself together, because he was the leader of this procession.

While other family members held and comforted each other, there was no one to hold and comfort Su Nim. Hundreds of miles away, he called me, so wrought with grief from losing the two family members who cared for him most, and there I was, in an entirely different country, unable to do anything. To this day, I'm not sure why I didn't just pack up and go to Korea. Perhaps it was the fear of going back and still not being able to be together. As painful as it was to be without him in Japan, I knew it would be even harder to be without him in Korea.

———

Unable to bear the loneliness I felt any longer, I befriended a Japanese man in my English class, and I ended up dating him. I thought it would take away my pain, but it just added to it, so eventually, I broke it off. By then, Su Nim was living in Seoul and finally had a phone to call me. That's when I told him about this man.

"I'm sorry," I cried, feeling horribly guilty.

"No, it's my fault. I was away from you. Don't worry, we will figure this out," he promised.

I really wanted to figure things out too, but I had committed to staying in Japan for two full years, and I knew that if I were to survive, I would have to start living and experiencing where I *was*— not where I hoped to be. I realized that though I could continue to welcome Su Nim's calls and letters, I had to stop waiting for them. I had to stop hinging my happiness on my interactions with Su Nim. Life was happening in the here and now, and I was missing it.

So during my second year in Japan, I got busy.

I joined a gym. I started studying Japanese with a private teacher. I climbed Mount Fuji.

Through it all, I continued to keep up with my daily meditation practice and spent my vacations at a meditation center in Kyoto. During one ten-day silent course there, I once again experienced the full realization—if only temporary—that I was a part of everything. And with that came the understanding that I was not separate from Su Nim, because he was part of everything too.

Visits from my parents and best friend, Lena, also helped. Playing tour guide was good medicine: I realized that I hadn't just been marking time in Japan. I was making progress. When I'd first arrived, I was so afraid of doing anything. Now, here I was, calling hotels and making reservations in Japanese. I had figured out train systems, menus, and great places to visit.

I was also making friends. I started hanging out with Mina, a new assistant at the school where I worked, and several of my students. I still didn't know what would happen between Su Nim and me, but at least I was living my life again. I had been walking around with blinders on for so long. I had been afraid to look at beauty that was all around me.

One day, I even finally had the courage to say something other than *"Konichiwa"* to the old man living behind my apartment. While he was cutting fresh flowers from his garden, I bravely burst out with *"Kyou wa ii tenki desu ne!"* (The weather is nice today!)—to which he replied, *"So desu ne! Ii tenki desu ne!"* (Yes! The weather is nice!) Then, suddenly, he handed me a bundle of the fresh-cut flowers over the fence.

In that moment, all the Japanese I hoped to test out on the old man left me. His gesture touched me deeply and opened me up. I had been closed off from this flow of love during most of my time in Japan. My world had been cast in a dark hue because of my unwillingness to accept my circumstances. I realized that the ability to feel happiness and love doesn't depend on person, place, or circumstance; it depends on a person's openness to what is already there for the offering. It was just how Su Nim described his realization with the farmer's wife and her potato pancake: We are never truly alone, because love is all around us. If we can realize that, we can tap into it at any time.

Lesson Six:

Know When It's Time to Let Go

"If you love someone, set them free."

—RICHARD BACH

I N MARCH, I was on my way back to Korea.

I couldn't believe it: Once I'd gotten comfortable being on my own, Su Nim was coming back into my life. Near the end of my time in Japan, we had resolved to be together again. We were done with the long-distance thing. But Korea was just a stopover this time. We were going to travel to the United States.

This was a big step for us as a couple—but an even bigger step for Su Nim, who would be meeting my extended family for the first time. My sister was planning to get married in April, so the whole family would be in Tennessee for her wedding.

At the Seoul arrivals terminal, I found Su Nim waiting for me in full monk garb. I walked past everyone else and straight into his arms—I didn't even care if anyone was watching as we embraced. I was just so happy to see him.

On the bus ride to the airport, Su Nim asked me how it felt to be arriving in Korea again after two years.

"It feels different this time," I said. "I don't know why."

"Because it is different," he offered. "You are different. I am different. We have changed."

I really wanted to believe that. In fact, I held on to those words like they were my life raft in a raging sea of uncertainty. As soon as the bus driver turned out the lights in the cabin, Su Nim reached over and held my hand. Warmth filled my body; I so missed his touch. During our long ride into the city, I wanted nothing more than to sit there in silence with this feeling.

To celebrate our reunion, we'd booked a couple of nights at the Hyatt in advance, and Su Nim had already checked us in. As we entered the lobby and went to the elevator together, no one seemed to care, even though he was dressed in robes. In any case, I didn't have the same anxiousness about it anymore. We had been through too much to care what others thought.

When we got to the room, Su Nim started to draw a bath. He kissed me while he peeled off my traveling clothes, and then he disrobed (literally). He stepped into the water, sat down, and leaned back against the tub. I followed suit and sat down between his legs, leaning back on his chest.

"I love you," he said, holding me in the warm water.

I couldn't answer. I was already crying.

"It's okay," he assured. "You made it here. We are together now."

We continued to soak in silence. After a time, Su Nim got out and grabbed two big towels. He wrapped one around himself and dried me off with the other, wrapping it around me in an embrace when he was done. Then we lay back on the bed and just held each other there. I felt my breath; I could hear the water drip in the tub and the *tick-tock* of Su Nim's watch. I stared into his dark eyes and then slowly studied his face, recalling all that I had missed—his brown skin, his bald head, his warm smile. I wanted to freeze the moment.

When he finally kissed me, I closed my eyes and let go. We moved together in silence, and once again, I returned to that place of no self. I could not define the space around me or the space around Su Nim. There was just energy, just love.

———

At the Seattle airport, my mom was surprised to see me in a red, billowy, Korean *hanbok* (skirt and tailored jacket) and my boyfriend in a long, gray robe. (This was probably even more curious for the other Americans in the airport, but I didn't care anymore—this was my town, and I'd wear whatever I wanted to wear . . . and I encouraged Su Nim to do the same.) I had picked up the gorgeous *hanbok* set in a traditional neighborhood in Seoul before we left for the States. It was a casual version, made from hand-dyed, quilted fabric.

I had lived in Asia for almost five years. And while I did visit home on vacations, I seemed to have become more accustomed to Asian life. The first thing that struck me was the *enormity* of everything. The trees in Seattle looked monstrous; the houses looked like palaces; the streets were wide, and there was space to move. I was used to tight quarters; concrete, beehive-like apartments; mass transportation; and crushing overpopulation.

If this was shocking to me—even after having visited home so many times during my vacations—I couldn't imagine how shocking it was for Su Nim. On the ride back to my parent's house, he hardly said a word, choosing to stare out the window at everything around him instead.

We were exhausted from the long flight. My mom wasn't sure what the sleeping arrangements should be, so she had a futon on the floor in one room and a double bed made up for me in the other room. But as we were preparing for sleep, she turned to us and said, "Oh, why don't you just share a room."

So we slept together in my childhood room. My yearbooks from high school were on the bookshelf, along with several framed photos—a picture of me in a Girl Scout uniform, a family photo taken at Christmas, and a couple pictures of family vacations. Su Nim picked each one up and studied it.

"It looks like you had a nice time," he said finally.

Su Nim had not been as fortunate. He grew up in Tongyeong— a fishing village located on the very southern tip of the Korean peninsula—and was raised by his grandparents. They all shared one bedroom between them. My parents' house was quite modest compared to most of the houses in the neighborhood, but to him, it was palatial.

In fact, to Su Nim, my childhood bed was so large and high off the ground that he was actually scared he might fall out of it. (In Korea, most people slept very low to the ground or on a *yo*.) I kissed him, and said, "Don't worry, you won't fall out. I'll be holding on to you all night." We got comfortable under the covers, and within minutes, we were fast asleep. But when I awoke in the morning, I found him sleeping on the bedroom floor, without even a blanket to cover him.

Despite his jet lag and all this newness, Su Nim was a good sport. He followed along with the program, was willing to try new things, and did his best to communicate with people around him. I knew it took guts to travel here with me, leaving behind everything that was familiar.

I also knew that Su Nim had it in his head that if he went all the way to the States with me and met my entire family, then he'd be almost committed to marrying me.

I had to admit, I was hoping this visit would end up in a proposal. Surely, after sleeping in my childhood bedroom, hanging out with my family, touring my neighborhood, and meeting my friends, he would be ready to cast aside his robes for good and be with me, right? And don't forget, there was my sister's wedding in Tennessee—maybe the wedding vibe would rub off on us. . . .

These thoughts filled my mind during our days together in the States. Yet whenever I brought the subject up, however delicately, he would skirt around it, finding something else to talk about.

The fact was, I was doing everything I could think of to make sure we stayed together. I was holding on to this love as tight as I could.

———————

In the past several years, I had traversed the entire South Korean peninsula, and I knew Su Nim's country quite well. Now it was his turn to learn about my country, and I was so excited to show it to him.

But Su Nim already felt like he knew enough about the United States. He'd seen his share of Western movies, so he thought he knew the drill: Everyone had a gun, and there was a lot of sex being had. (Thank you, Hollywood!)

It was an impression that proved hard to shake, despite my best efforts. When we decided to take a road trip down the West Coast to a ten-day Vipassana course in Fresno, California, he questioned my plan to camp along the way.

"Is it safe?" he asked.

"Of course it's safe," I laughed. "We'll be in the wilderness with other happy campers,"—as if Ranger Rick and Yogi Bear would be at the next campsite over. I told him how we'd roast marshmallows, make s'mores, sing campfire songs, and have a jolly-good time.

And we did. We stayed at pristine campgrounds right along the coast, cooked our food over a fire pit, watched the sun go down, and fell asleep to the sound of the fire still crackling outside the tent.

But one night, on the trip back, at a campground by the Golden Gate Bridge, I woke up to see flashing red lights outside our tent.

"Su Nim, wake up! I think the cops are here!" I whispered, shaking him.

I heard an officer approach the tent next to ours. "You have the right to remain silent," he said.

I peeped through the tent flap and watched as two officers hauled a scruffy-looking fellow away in handcuffs.

Good god, we were sleeping next to a criminal! I thought. *Maybe he was a bank robber, or a child molester, or mass-murderer!* My mind was reeling. My heart was pumping.

"Relax, everything is fine," said Su Nim drowsily. "We are safe, remember? We are in a family campground. Go back to sleep."

Boy had he changed his tune.

As for me, I decided that would be the last night we stayed in a campground. I phoned a friend in San Francisco, and he agreed to let us crash on his couch. While there, we did all the tourist stuff— Haight-Ashbury, Fishermen's Wharf, Chinatown—before heading back to Washington . . . staying in hotels the rest of the way.

By the time we made it to my parents' house, my sister's wedding was almost upon us. It would be the first time most of my family and friends would meet Su Nim. Upon our arrival in Tennessee and after checking into a hotel, my sister and her soon-to-be husband, David, picked us up for, of all things, laser tag. Yes, that was Su Nim's first outing with my sister and her future husband. All my intoning that life in America was nothing like the movies, and here we sat: an entire wedding party outfitted in laser vests with guns at our sides.

"So everyone make sure your vests are securely attached by fastening the strap around your waist," our guide instructed. I looked to see what Su Nim thought of all of this, but he was just taking it all in. "Now, when you want to attack your opponent, you need to aim and shoot right for this section of the vest," he said, pointing to his heart. "When it lights up, it's an indication that you've hit your target."

Holy cow! All I wanted to do was turn off my vest and hide under a table.

Just then, the instructor gave the signal, and the war was on. I immediately disappeared behind a curtain to wait this thing out— and I fully expected Su Nim to follow suit. Instead, he jumped right into the battle and started taking out friends and family members one by one. He was good. Like James Bond good.

I may have been shocked by his behavior, but after that afternoon, it was clear that Su Nim had won everyone's heart.

The next day, my sister informed us that her bachelorette party would be held at a nearby family restaurant. Su Nim, however, would be heading to Hooters with the boys.

Uh-oh, I thought. *More proof that the movies weren't kidding.*

"What's Hooters?" Su Nim asked.

"Um, we'll let the guys tell you about that," I answered.

So while I watched my sister unwrap garter belts and thongs, Su Nim sat in a pickup between two guys dressed like cowboys to go see some hooters. But I soon realized that I should be grateful: As far as most bachelor parties go in America, eating spicy chicken wings and drinking beer at Hooters is pretty tame.

When Su Nim arrived back at the hotel, I asked him if he had a good time.

"Yes, but I expected more than that," he said. "They were just women with big boobs. Who cares? That's not like the bachelor parties I saw in the movies."

The next day, before the wedding, a discussion ensued on what the monk would wear to the wedding. I was one of the bridesmaids, so my attire had been predetermined.

"I think he should just wear his long monk robe," my mom said.

I could just see it now. My sister's Tennessean in-laws would be aghast. The wedding was traditional. People were going to be wearing traditional wedding clothes. The focus was supposed to be on the bride. What would happen if a man with a shaved head and a robe showed up? Sure, I had encouraged Su Nim to wear whatever he wanted to in America, but this was different. This day was for my sister and her husband. I would have worn a Victorian ball gown with a bustle had my sister asked.

"Um, maybe David has something—a shirt or a tie—that Su Nim could wear."

"Yes, I'm sure Su Nim could wear one of his shirts and a tie. He probably has an extra jacket too," my sister replied, relieved that I had offered up the idea.

Even though the jacket was so big it threatened to engulf Su Nim, the day was saved. Now, at least, he sort of blended in.

The wedding was in a quaint little church, and the reception was held in a beautiful old Southern mansion and featured a swing band. The band took a break for the cake-cutting and the bouquet-tossing. And who do you think caught it? Yep. You guessed it. But if you believe the pictures of the toss, I took out several members of the wedding party in my single-minded pursuit. (Perhaps as a punishment, I was stabbed by a pin sticking out of the bouquet, causing me to bleed throughout the rest of the reception.)

The next day, we headed to Florida with my father and stepmom. My father is a very generous and kind person by nature, but I doubt that Su Nim was the person my father imagined his eldest daughter being with. Despite his paternal doubts, my father and stepmother showed us a lovely time. Su Nim even found a Korean grocery store and prepared a feast for the four of us as his parting gift.

I was happy that he had a chance to meet most of my family, and that they got along well. But I secretly hoped that it also meant he was ready to be with me, for better or for worse.

———————

Back at my mom's house, I became consumed with trying to figure out how we could stay in America. I couldn't bear having Su Nim return to Korea without me, and I wasn't sure I wanted to live in Asia anymore. I called the embassy and found out details of how we could get married and stay.

Su Nim was uneasy about this though. After all, neither of us had jobs or much money left. What would we do in the States? Particularly, what would Su Nim do? He had never held a job before. This was all too much for him. One afternoon, when I was going over the plan I had for him to stay with me, he said, "The time does not seem right. I need to go back to Korea."

My heart sank like a stone. I knew he was right, but I was still intent on making it work somehow. After hours of discussion, we decided it was easier for me to go back to Korea and get a job there than for Su Nim to stay in America and try to find work. It's what made the most sense. But more than that, I knew he was still conflicted about us: He wasn't ready to let go of his monk life, or me.

Su Nim left for Korea in early June, and I immediately got to work on finding a teaching position there. I was so motivated that I got accepted to teach at five colleges and had to choose between them.

I finally picked a college near Seoul, figuring that it was centrally located, and that somehow, Su Nim would be able to find a temple gig close to me. It all seemed rational at the time, yet in retrospect, it was simply insane. Here I was, throwing myself right back into the situation I had so desperately wanted to escape. I was marching straight back into a life of living separately from Su Nim. Of hiding out and never being free to love each other openly. A life that had left me emotionally torn.

———

Su Nim was pretty despondent when he left for Korea. The fact that he could not support me or make a life with me made him depressed. I could see how it was easier to go back to the life he always knew, even if it broke his heart and tugged at his conscience.

When I arrived in Korea's sweltering heat, it had been five years— almost to the day—since I first arrived in the country. After Su Nim's visit to the States, I believed that somehow things would be different this time. I believed that we would finally figure it out, like Su Nim had promised in the past.

Instead, it felt like he was giving up—like he had exhausted all the possibilities to be with me, and it just wouldn't work out.

He didn't meet me at the airport. In fact, I didn't see him until several weeks after I had settled into my new job and life. When we did finally did start meeting, he could only see me sporadically. He had things to do at the temple and was busy most of the time. And when we were together, he didn't want to talk about our relationship. He just wanted to be with me in the moment.

"How is this going to work with you living in the monastery and never knowing when you can see me? I feel like we are still hiding out," I said one night.

"Well, I'm here now, aren't I? I moved to the monastery in Seoul to be close to you. We are together now, and that's the most important thing, isn't it? I can't be sure when we can meet again, but we will," he replied.

"I just feel like not much has changed. After all we've been through, I thought things would be different," I said.

"It's not so easy, Kathy," was his response. "What am I supposed to do? I am a monk. It is not so easy to change."

As much as I hated to admit it, he was clearly not ready to be with me completely. He was still struggling with our relationship and was unable to make a firm decision. Both his monk life and I were equally important to him, but having both in his life also caused us both a great deal of suffering.

So I made the decision for him. Since he wasn't ready to sever his ties with the monastery, I made it easy for him to sever his ties with me: I broke it off. Completely.

As painful as it was to let go, I knew it was the right thing for both of us: He and I had been trapped in the back-and-forth pattern of this relationship for years now: We needed, deserved, to be set free. And since he didn't intend to let go, it had to be me.

If it wasn't going to work out with Su Nim, I knew that I had to be totally clear that it was over.

"Listen, I can't see you anymore. It's just too hard," I told him over the phone one day, too afraid that if I tried to tell him in person I would not be able to say these words.

I bit my lip and tried to hold back from bursting out in tears. I tried to remain cool and collected, but my heart was pounding in my throat. I was shaking.

After a long pause, he finally said, "I understand; can we meet?"

"No, we can't meet. I gotta go." And I hung up.

I knew this probably wasn't the most mature way of handling the situation, but I knew the conversation by heart now—and knew it never ended decisively once we began to talk about things. I had to be strong, for both of us.

Numb for weeks after that, I moped around in a daze. I tried to carry on with my life, but was starting to wonder what the point of my life in Korea was now that Su Nim was gone.

During that difficult time, I put all my energy into the Vipassana practice I had started while in Nepal with Su Nim. Helping to organize the first Vipassana course in South Korea gave me a reason to stay there. Meditation helped me find myself again. It gave me the strength to remember that my own well-being was important, and that I should continue to nurture it. I needed to be able to stand on my own two feet and know who I was without Su Nim. As painful as that was, I knew that was what I needed to do.

I learned, perhaps the hard way, that you can't hold on to love. That the tighter your grip, the more it slips through your fingers. It might be the hardest lesson I've had to learn, but it is indeed true: If you really love someone, you have to be willing to let them go, to set them free—and that by doing so, you're freeing yourself as well.

....

Surrender to the Unknown

"The way of the heart is the way of courage.
It is to live in insecurity; it is to live in love,
and trust; it is to move in the unknown."
—OSHO

AND WHAT DO you know: Once I surrendered completely and let go of the reigns, my love came galloping back into my life. Once he was finally completely freed from *having* to make a choice, it became clear to him which life he wanted.

He showed up in his robes on the doorstep of my apartment. A backpack slung over his shoulder and containing all of his earthly possessions was an indicator that he wasn't just dropping by for a visit.

I'd finally gotten the hang of being on my own. But now that he was standing there in front of me, I trembled. I was scared to let him in, but I couldn't bring myself to shut the door on him either.

"Can I come in?" he asked.

I nodded.

He threw his backpack down and hugged me, then stepped back and looked at me. I was crying, and he wiped each tear from my face as they rolled down my cheeks. I pulled away, went into the bedroom, and dropped down onto the bed. He cautiously followed, stretching out next to me. We stared at the ceiling.

"I left the temple," he said. "I'm not going back."

It was the first time he had ever said these words. He seemed serious, but I was scared of returning to the life we had before. After surviving years of our on-again, off-again relationship, I didn't know if I had it in me to believe him.

"How can I be sure about that?" I said.

He said nothing. And then, after a long time, I murmured, "What will you do?"

"I could sell vegetables and rice on the side of the road!" he exclaimed with newly found enthusiasm.

Oh god! I thought. I imagined myself standing barefoot, knee-high in a rice field, my back bent and my face tanned from all those days of hard labor. I envisioned Su Nim, thin as a rail, waving down the rare car that dared venture along the desolate road. This was not what I had planned for my life. There had to be another way.

As it turned out, Su Nim had never officially told the temple he was going. He just left. I didn't question this. After all, they'd understand. They were all practicing nonattachment, right? The truth is, it wasn't unheard of for monks to leave the monastery in Korea. Like Su Nim, many had joined when they were young. It wasn't unusual for their life circumstances or views to change as they got older. They were human, just like the rest of us. They could change their minds. Su Nim never met with his master before leaving the monastery, but I believe he probably knows what happened. After my meeting with his master years ago, I couldn't imagine he'd be angry. He didn't seem to have an angry bone in his body.

So I let Su Nim in. Not just into my apartment, but into my life. Not for an afternoon or evening, but to stay. He changed his name back to the one given at his birth, Seong Yoon, which was later shortened even further to Yoon, for the sake of simplicity. He tied up his monk robes in a large piece of silk and placed them at the bottom of the closet in my apartment.

So that was it.

Though it took me a while to really believe that he was here for good, the fact that he now wore regular clothes was an indication that he was serious. Plus, we were no longer hiding out in public— even though we were in Korea. We kissed and held hands on the busy sidewalks surrounding my apartment. We went on dates, and I even invited some of my coworkers around to the apartment to play cards.

We were a couple—finally.

But I had already made plans to meet my family for Christmas in New York, and to stay in the States until early February. So once again, we had to part ways.

Before leaving, I urged him to try to find a job in my absence. He didn't have any money. In fact, I found out later that he ate cabbage and miso soup the entire time I was gone. He was determined to find work though, and while I was away, he got a job as a waiter at a sushi restaurant. It was not really the career transition I had imagined for him, but hey, it was a job.

One day in January, I called him from Seattle and asked how work was going.

"I didn't go," he said. "I quit."

As it turned out, Seong Yoon was a terrible waiter. He fouled up everyone's order. One patron felt so sorry for him that he left a large tip, so sure he wouldn't last another day. So he quit as soon as he received his first paycheck.

But he didn't give up on work: He posted signs around the apartment building offering to teach yoga, which he had mastered while at the monastery. It worked: Two Canadian English teachers and a few Koreans responded to the ad, and soon, my living room was full of yoga mats and people in stretch pants listening to soothing music while Seong Yoon fumbled his way through instructions in both English and Korean.

Upon my return, I joined in on the classes myself. Despite the language difficulties, he seemed to have a knack for teaching. I was so happy he found a job that suited him.

After a couple months of teaching yoga in my apartment, he was intent on starting a yoga business. But I was having trouble seeing how this dream would become a reality. We didn't have any money to start a business, and neither of us had any formal training. Didn't we need training? Certification?

Not to mention that neither of us had ever run a business in our lives. Seong Yoon hadn't even managed to hold onto his first and only job for more than a couple weeks. It seemed like a rather large leap of faith to make. Then again, leaving the monastery was the biggest leap of Seong Yoon's life—after that, it probably seemed to him that there was nothing he couldn't do.

One afternoon in early March, Seong Yoon called me. "I found a building!" he exclaimed. But we needed $10,000 for a deposit. We just didn't have that kind of money. So I took a deep breath and picked up the telephone and called my dad.

Ever since I was a child, it had been hard for me to ask my parents for money. I was, and am, fiercely independent, but this was an all-or-nothing sort of deal, and we needed to make a decision quick.

I explained my story and then said, "So, Dad, can we borrow ten thousand dollars to start a business?"

I held my breath. I could only imagine what must have been going through my father's head at that moment. Here was his daughter, with a recent ex-monk boyfriend, wanting a large sum of money to start a yoga business in a faraway country. Any father would have been hesitant.

After a short silence, he said, "I want to help you, so I will do it. How soon do you need it, and where do I send it?"

I started breathing again.

———————

We signed contracts, hired electricians, put in floors, covered the walls in rice paper, designed logos, changed lights, created a website, and bought a credit card machine.

And, in the midst of all of this, Seong Yoon found out that he had been accepted to a six-week yoga teacher's training program at a yoga college in India. While his master had trained him in yoga in the monastery, Seong Yoon knew that most people attending yoga classes in South Korea wanted to learn from a teacher who had studied formally at a reputable school. So he decided to go, realizing that it would be important for the success of his school.

He'd have to leave soon though, and there was still so much to be done with the studio if we were going to open on time. I wasn't sure I could figure things out on my own, with my broken Korean. Once again, doubt gripped me.

"How is this going to work out?" I worried.

"It will," Seong Yoon said. "It always does."

His great faith was soon put to the test—and once again, he passed. One day before he was supposed to leave, Seong Yoon popped over to the Indian embassy to pick up his visa. When he got to the front of the line, a scholarly looking Indian man peered down at him through his reading spectacles and said, "What is dee purpose of your treep?"

"I'm going to attend a yoga teacher's training course," Seong Yoon replied.

"Sir, you need a student visa for that. It takes one month."

"But I have a plane ticket to India for tomorrow."

"Sir, this is impossible. You cannot go tomorrow. You need to wait for a student visa."

There was silence. Seong Yoon and this Indian man just stood there, staring at each other. What could be done? If I had been there (thank goodness I wasn't), I probably would have shouted. But Seong Yoon just closed his eyes for a moment and let everything go.

And then he said, "Sir, I was really hoping to be on that flight tomorrow to India. I am going for my spirit. I'm going for spirituality. That's why people go to India, right? They go for a spiritual experience. I don't want to miss this chance."

The Indian man stood there listening to Seong Yoon. He never took his eyes off of him. The only difference was in his stare. Instead of a hard glare, his eyes had softened a bit. He looked down at Seong Yoon's passport and hesitated. He seemed to be pondering something.

"Okay, my friend, I'll change," he said.

And right there, with a few pen strokes, he changed the "T" on Seong Yoon's visa to an "S."

"Have a good trip to India, my friend, and may you find what you are looking for."

———————

The next morning, Seong Yoon was gone. I had to deal with a faulty electrical system. I had to haggle in my limited Korean with the sign-shop owner. Luckily, I had a few Korean friends to help me out. But for most of the six weeks while Seong Yoon was gone, the school sat empty. There wasn't much I could do until he came back.

It was May 2002, and the World Cup soccer craze had begun. Everyone in the country was so proud that South Korea was hosting the tournament, and the whole city was charged with a collective energy. During matches, South Koreans gathered on the front stoops of shops, watching the game on tiny TVs. Every single sports bar was overflowing.

One evening, during the height of the tournament, I was walking down a tiny path between the towering fifteen-story buildings that made up my apartment complex. I was on my way home from the grocery store, and it felt so odd on this warm night that no one else was on the path. Of course, everyone was inside—their eyes glued to the TV.

Suddenly, the ground began to shake. *Are we having an earthquake?* I wondered. And then it occurred to me that the South Koreans must have just scored, because the entire apartment complex exploded in cheers, chanting *"Dae-han-min-guk!"* (South Korea!) over and over again.

While I was in Korea, lost in a sea of red jerseys, Seong Yoon was warding off rats from his sleeping bag at a sweltering ashram outside of Bombay. There were seven foreigners attending the program—two from France, one from Italy, one from Slovenia, one from Thailand, one from Japan, and Seong Yoon—and no one understood a lick of what was discussed in the classroom. The Indian-accented English was indecipherable. At one point, one of the French women went to the director of the program and demanded her money back.

"We paid money to learn yoga theory, and we have no idea what our teachers are saying. How can we continue?"

"Don't worry, my friend, you will all get certificates in the end."

So everyone suffered through theory, looking forward to the actual mat practice. At least that should be pretty easy to figure out. While Indians and Koreans alike revered this yoga program, Seong Yoon's notebook was full of doodles. The language barrier and the oppressive heat made concentration nearly impossible. Yet somehow, he made it through, certificate in hand.

I made it through too. But those six weeks couldn't have come to an end fast enough. A week before Seong Yoon was to arrive home, I couldn't do anything but think about his return. I imagined he'd be so relaxed and radiant after spending six weeks in a yoga ashram.

I went by bus to meet him at the airport. I stood there with dozens of other Koreans, most of them donning red jerseys, waiting for the passengers to emerge through the double doors of security.

I had to blink a few times to make sure I was seeing correctly. Yes, there he was. No soccer jersey for him, though. He stepped through the security gate looking like Gandhi. He was wearing white cotton pants that puffed out at the waist and tapered in at the calves. Over that, he wore a long, white, flowing shirt. He folded his hands in *namaste* to greet me. Koreans stared. It was nerve-wracking enough when he was wearing monk garb with his American girlfriend, but now he looked like a guru.

He walked straight over to me and said, *"Namaste, namaste!"*

"Whoa. What's that you are wearing?"

"Oh, these are my lovely Indian clothes. Don't I look like a sannyasin?"

"Yes, you do," I said. I was feeling little uncomfortable with the fact that I was wearing shorts and a T-shirt with the holy Korean man from India.

When we got back to my apartment, Seong Yoon dumped out the contents of his backpack onto the floor. There were soaps, incense, paintings, statues, oils, shawls, and beautiful Indian clothes for me, so that we could match. I tried the different outfits on; they were beautiful.

"Did you practice yoga while you were there, or did you just shop?" I inquired with a smile.

"You know, I really didn't understand what they were talking about in the classroom, so I wasn't really into it. I enjoyed the actual yoga practice time, and I got a lot from the reading material, but the rest of the time, I just tried to enjoy myself. So, yes, I shopped a little and ate sweet mangoes from the market."

"Sounds nice," I said.

"It was nice, but it's even nicer to be with you. I missed you."

He reached over and pulled me into his arms.

We spent a few days together without thinking too much about what we needed to do to get the school ready for its grand opening.

But soon, there was less than a week until showtime, and the sign still wasn't up. Seong Yoon called the sign shop, and they promised to have the crane ready to lift it up by the next day.

It was thrilling to watch the crane hoist up our ten-foot sign that read OM SHANTI YOGA SCHOOL in English and Korean. The street was crowded with people who all stopped to gawk at the action, chattering among themselves about the fact that there was going to be a yoga school in their neighborhood.

We went to a nearby sports bar to celebrate. Seong Yoon was still wearing his Indian garb. (Once he finds clothes he likes, he tends to wear them until they practically fall off. I often wonder if this is a habit left over from his monastic days, where wardrobe selection was, of course, pretty limited.) The sports bar was crowded. We ordered some appetizers, and Seong Yoon decided he wanted a beer to celebrate. Carrying on a conversation was a challenge with the soccer match on, however. As we were going over the plans for our opening, Seong Yoon sprung from his chair, fist in the air, and yelled, *"Dae-han-min-guk!"* Korea had just scored. It was official; he had been hypnotized too. Soon after, he traded in his Ghandi outfit for a Korean Red Devils jersey.

On the morning of the grand opening, we woke up and put on our matching Indian outfits. Seong Yoon was wearing his airport-arrival clothes, and I sported an intricately embroidered, rose-pink *shalwar kameez*, an Indian outfit with puffy pants and a long, dress-like shirt. For the finishing touch, I draped a matching pink shawl around my shoulders. Heading out of the apartment complex looking like a pair of Bollywood extras, we walked arm and arm down the path as people whispered and pointed, wondering what sort of mischief we were up to.

We headed to the neighborhood market to pick up our order of *dukk* (Korean rice cake), a treat that's always served at grand openings in South Korea. Dancing girls were also usually part of the package, but we decided to skip them. Instead, we asked a fellow yoga teacher to give a speech. He too was clad in Indian clothes. Among the guests were a few psychologists who I privately tutored in English; a professor from the college where I taught; and several fellow teachers, students, friends, neighbors, and random people from the community who had heard about the studio. It was a fantastic turnout. As per the custom in Korea, we received many large plants in porcelain pots. There was a palm tree, an orchid, a dracaena tree (known as a "lucky tree" in Korea), and a few houseplants. We meditated, listened to a lecture, and even practiced a bit of yoga before diving into the feast of *dukk*, fruit, tea, and juice. There was a lot of clapping, cheering, congratulating, bowing, and handshaking that day. I felt like the school was already an instant success.

But we weren't an instant success. The opening was great, but attendance was low. Very low. Some days, no one showed up. During the first week, I believe we had three students. I worried we'd go belly up before we even started.

"Oh god, what have we done? How are we going to pay the rent?" I said.

Seong Yoon had no idea either. But he was not going to quit. He gave all he had to those few students that came. And slowly, things improved.

When I left that summer to attend my own month-long yoga teacher's training course in Colorado, he had about ten students. Since I wasn't sure we had the money to hire more yoga teachers, I thought I should at least train myself. I couldn't really be picky about which school I attended—I just needed a certificate and a program that would fit into the timeframe that I had. The course I chose was at a yoga ashram, and I hadn't really read up on the literature, so I didn't know what to expect. I knew the program was recognized by Yoga Alliance, an internationally recognized professional organization. So I just decided to be open to whatever awaited me . . . and boy, was that more than I bargained for.

A woman in a flowing sari greeted me. "Hi, I'm Karuna. Welcome. Are you here for the teacher's training course?"

"Yes, I am."

"Well, Sati will check you in."

Why does everyone have funky names? I wondered.

"Hi, I'm Sati, welcome," she said—apparently to me, but staring off into space.

She was so slow getting my paperwork, room number, and books organized that I was sure the course would be over before she was done.

During orientation, I learned we'd have to get up at the crack of dawn, put on our saris, dresses, or skirts, and hike our way through the dark to the temple, where we were required to sit on the floor for over an hour and recite the entire Bhagavad Gītā. We'd also have three meals a day, yoga practice, and classes that include yoga theory, anatomy, and Sanskrit. We could attend any of the onsite yoga and deep-relaxation classes in the evening. On weekends, when the guru came to town, we were expected to be there.

Guru? I didn't know there would be a guru! The first weekend he showed up, we all were required to meet for a fire ceremony. For hours we sat on the floor, throwing rice into a pit of fire while chanting, *"Om nama shivaya svaha."* It was dark, and the fire's glow lit up everyone's faces. It felt a little eerie, and I was getting dizzy from chanting for so long.

The guru—a large man with Italian roots from New York City—sat in what looked like a throne. His twinkling eyes made him look a bit like Santa Claus. At the end of the ceremony, everyone formed a line to be blessed by the guru. Reaching down from his throne, he carefully scooped up some smoldering coals from the fire and placed them next to him. One by one, the devotees lined up to receive his blessing—a smudge of coal on their forehead. Once they'd been "blessed," the people fell back, as if they had just been miraculously healed.

Um . . . this wasn't what I signed up for. I thought. *I'm here to get trained in yoga, not to become a cult member.* I could have done without the dancing around with umbrellas and mirrors, the drumming, the anointing, and the smudging of coal between my eyebrows, but I was there, so I surrendered to it. Besides, I needed the certificate.

While I was leaping around, trying and failing to feel the bliss, Seong Yoon was back in South Korea, staring out of his new yoga-school window for much of the day, wondering when the crowd of yogis and yoginis was going to show up.

"So, are you learning lots of yoga?" he asked when I called. He sounded miles away. I sat in the dining hall in a rocking chair, using the only public pay phone. I was surrounded by a bunch of impatient yogis.

"I'm learning that I don't want to live in a yoga ashram, and that I like the name my parents gave me."

"What does that mean?"

"I'll tell you later," I said. "So, are you getting more students?"

"Well, it's going a little slow. There are many days when no one shows up. But I'm taking it one day at a time. I'm trying to just be in the moment and feel myself."

"Yes, I hear you there," I said.

"But don't worry. Everything is going to be okay" was the last thing I heard before a dial tone. I must have used up my phone card.

So I hung up, went back to my bunk, put on my sari, and got ready for another drum session at the temple of bliss.

————————

After I returned to Korea, I made it a point to attend one of Seong Yoon's classes as soon as possible. He had informed me that things had improved in the last couple of weeks. Boy, was that was an understatement: I showed up to a full house. There was barely enough space for all the students.

Since I had just returned from my training course, I was sure the class would be a piece of cake for me. I was wrong. Seong Yoon brought the students to their edge—and then made them feel what it was like to be at that edge. I was holding my ankles in *danurasana* (bow pose) for more than a minute before I collapsed flat on my mat—well before he'd given the signal to release the pose. The other students, however, had held it the whole time with no problem.

It's not that *danurasana* is difficult—it's not. It's that the series of postures that led up to that point already had me sweating and wishing I could run back to my apartment, sit on the sofa under a blanket, and eat chocolate. I was out of my comfort zone. I was right there, on the edge, with all the other students, and none of them looked like they wanted to run. What had I been doing the entire time at the ashram? I spent my time leaping around to drum music, chanting, fussing around with my sari, throwing rice into fire—but did I ever really experience yoga? Because right there, in that room full of yoga students, I felt like I was practicing yoga for the first time.

He didn't talk incessantly through his class, like the yoga teachers did back in the States. He let each student have their own experience of the practice. His years of yoga and meditation in the monastery gave him a different reference point as a teacher. He didn't pussyfoot around with bells, whistles, drums, and gongs. Like a Zen master with a big stick, he guided his students straight inside. There was nothing to do but face what was there.

Just as I thought I had reached my edge, emotionally and physically, Seong Yoon had us letting go of it all in *savasana* (corpse pose). Instead of guiding us through this resting portion of the class, he put on some soft music, had us all cover up with a blanket, and just let us be. At the end of the class, we came up to a seated position and did a little meditation. Then we all chanted "Om" three times, folded our hands together, and said "Namaste" in unison.

And that was the end of the class. I sat there in disbelief. Seong Yoon was a natural at teaching yoga. He had his own technique, and it was all his combined experience that led him to this. All of the students thanked him. Some stayed for tea and a chat. Others brought their friends, parents, and family members, eager to have them sign up for classes.

It spread like wildfire that there was a yoga master in the neighborhood, and people were eager to come and see for themselves.

Here he was—someone who had never held a job for more than two weeks—running a successful business. He succeeded by giving everything he had to what he was doing. It's no wonder the class was at its maximum capacity. The only wonder was that I ever doubted this.

Still, in the days that followed, the rational part of me started wondering how long he could sustain it. I wasn't quite as prepared as he was to surrender to whatever would be. I still felt the need to try to get things under control.

It would take time—and several more yoga classes with Seong Yoon, before I could rest more easily in the realm of the unknown. By bringing me to my edge (both in life and in yoga class) and then keeping me there, Seong Yoon taught me the art of surrender. The edge, I learned, is the best place to learn to accept the unknown. But being at the edge is not about pushing yourself—that's just another way of trying to assert control. Instead, being at the edge is about surrendering and allowing whatever is to be what it is—and then simply bearing witness to it.

In the beginning, I didn't like not knowing where this new path with the yoga business would lead. But the fact is, the future is always unknown. All we can do is keeping walking toward what we want and trusting that if we follow our hearts, everything will be okay. And besides, there's a bonus that comes with not knowing where you are going: The possibilities of where you might end up are endless.

You Are More Than the Roles You Play

The whole is greater than the sum of its parts.
—ARISTOTLE

B Y THE FOLLOWING fall, we decided to make it official. We decided to get married.

There wasn't a lot of fanfare around the proposal or engagement. It was simple, honest, and mutual—and after seven years of riding an emotional rollercoaster, that's exactly what I wanted. Seong Yoon didn't get down on his knees, hide an engagement ring in a cupcake, or serenade me outside my bedroom window. He just said, "Let's get married," then took me shopping and told me to pick out any ring I liked. I chose a simple, white-gold band with a tiny single diamond. It's unassuming, but it sparkles like nothing I've ever seen—just like Seong Yoon.

But I still hadn't met his family. I'd wanted to for a long time already, but whenever I brought up the idea, he immediately felt uneasy and tried to change the subject. It was a complicated situation: Seong Yoon's mother had gotten pregnant when she was only eighteen. His parents lived together out of wedlock until he was six. Then they got married and had another baby. Shortly after the arrival of his sister, Seong Yoon moved into his paternal grandparent's house to relieve his young mother's burden. (In Korea, it isn't unusual for grandparents to take on the responsibility of raising children.) When he was fourteen, his parents divorced, his sister joined him at their grandparents, and their mother was cast out of the family.

Historically, a divorce in Korea would usually result in the mother losing custody of her children. Out of shame, many women moved away and didn't return to see their children, opting to start new families instead. While there are currently more cases of women gaining custody of their children, Seong Yoon's mother was one of those women who opted to move away. So when Seong Yoon turned nineteen—as soon as he had graduated from high school and was old enough to leave Tongyeong—he left his hometown. In the years that followed he rarely visited, and he didn't speak to his father for a long time.

Now that we were getting married, he promised he would take me to meet his father's side of the family . . . but first he had to let them know about me. Imagine his father's surprise when, out of the blue, he receives a call from his son—who, after years of being in a monastery, is now informing him that he's marrying his American girlfriend, a relationship his father knew nothing about.

In Seong Yoon's village, Tongyeong—located as far south on the Korean peninsula as you can go—fishing boats dotted the harbor with little spots of color, and small islands were scattered off the coast, which stretched out wide in front of us. To get to his house, we wandered in and out of neighborhoods with dated apartment buildings and dilapidated houses. We walked past the bakery—where Seong Yoon used to meet his high school friends—and past the only pizza parlor in town. His house, it seemed, was the end of the road—in more ways than one.

"This is it!" Seong Yoon said excitedly.

"Where?" I said. All I saw in front of us was huge heap of trash.

"This is my house. This is where I grew up."

"This is a pile of trash. You couldn't have grown up here. Tell me you did *not* grow up here," I panicked.

"Not here," he assured me, "Behind the garbage. Do you see that door there?"

A door, falling off its hinges, was the entrance to what I wouldn't quite call a house. It might have been one at some point, but not anymore. The broken-down building had been divided in half to accommodate a computer game room, where high school kids could gather to meet their friends and while away the afternoon. Seong Yoon's father emerged from the shack, almost taking the door with him.

"Anyoung haseyo!" he said, greeting us.

"Anyoung haseyo," said Seong Yoon, and he introduced me.

He bowed. *"Bang gap sumnida!"* (Nice to meet you!)

I bowed back, not sure what to do, and less sure what to say in my limited Korean.

His father was nothing like I expected. While Seong Yoon was thin, with fine features and a very gentle nature, his father looked like he could have been a member of the Korean mafia. He was huge, and he wore a black leather gangster jacket and a black felt hat with a feather in it. When he smiled, I saw he was missing a few teeth.

"Come in, come in!" he entreated.

I cautiously made my way through the broken door, walking past a tiny kitchen with a sink full of dirty dishes. Seong Yoon's father ushered us into a room that seemed to serve as a living room, dining room, and bedroom. We sat down in a circle, but I couldn't help but feel that I was in his personal space. A box of tissue, a lamp, and a faded family photo in a broken frame sat on a bedside table. An antique black-lacquer Korean dresser adorned with intricate mother-of-pearl designs was against a far wall. Clothes hung from hooks on the wall above the dresser, which held stacks of old blankets. It looked like things hadn't been touched in the room since Seong Yoon lived there. The linoleum floor had radiant heat but was badly in need of repair. Seong Yoon and his father chatted a bit in Korean, and then a woman arrived with tea. She was a *dabang* woman. *Dabang* were coffeehouses primarily for men, staffed by women in revealing clothing who were obviously there to entertain the customers as well as wait on them. These ladies also made house calls.

I suppose it's stating the obvious to say that it was awkward sitting in this ramshackle room with Seong Yoon and his father—whom he hadn't seen in over three years—as a woman in a low-cut blouse and tight skirt served us tea. In fact, I couldn't help feeling like I was in a brothel. It certainly wasn't one of your more stereotypical meet-the-parents moments.

Now I understood why Seong Yoon didn't want me to visit his hometown. It was depressing.

His father pulled out a family album from a drawer and opened it. Even though he was just a boy, Seong Yoon looked so serious in the photos. He didn't smile. Actually, no one was smiling.

It was getting late, so Seong Yoon's father decided to accompany us on our walk into town. We were staying at a nearby love hotel—the only accommodations in the area. We walked through a long tunnel to get to town. It seemed to stretch for miles, and I was starting to wonder if we'd ever emerge from the other side of it. On our way through the tunnel, Seong Yoon's father turned to greet a weary-looking man lying on the side of the road under a pile of old blankets. He appeared to be homeless.

"*Anyoung haseyo,*" he said.

"*Anyoung haseyo,*" said a weak voice from under the blankets. As we neared the end of the tunnel, his father explained to us that this man was an old friend who he hadn't seen in ages. I wondered if we should go back and help the man out or offer him some food or something. But Seong Yoon and his father, now engrossed in a conversation, continued walking, and I reluctantly followed.

By the time we reached the end of the tunnel, I was completely depressed. When the road forked, we said our goodbyes to his father and started in the direction of our dingy hotel. Along the coastline road, fishermen worked on their boats, preparing for the next morning's outing. Right there, in the middle of street, I broke down. Tears filled my eyes and streaked down my cheeks.

"What's wrong?" Seong Yoon asked, worried.

"It's so sad. I don't know what I expected, but I felt so sad this afternoon."

Seong Yoon held me in the street while I sobbed.

"I didn't want to bring you here, but I knew you wanted to come," he said.

"Is this why you became a monk?" I asked.

"I didn't feel comfortable in my family," Seong Yoon explained. "I spent many of my high school days at a local temple. I felt safe there. I felt happy. But I did not feel these things at home."

"I can see why," I said.

"But I am not my family, so don't worry. I love you," Seong Yoon said.

He led me into our dingy hotel room. Once inside, we sat down on the edge of a musty bed in front of a picture window. Seong Yoon wrapped his arms around me and pulled my head into his chest and stroked my hair. We sat there in silence staring out at the harbor until the last flicker of sunlight dropped below the horizon. In those moments, lying there in my future husband's arms, I let go of the afternoon and just let myself be in that peace.

Seong Yoon's extended family wanted to treat us to a pre-wedding dinner in nearby Masan—your typical Korean city with an urban sprawl of cement apartment buildings and neon lights. His father, his sister, and all of his aunts, uncles, and cousins gathered together at a traditional restaurant situated in a quiet little cul-de-sac, well separated from the clamor and chaos of the city. We sat on the floor eating *bulgogi* (barbecued beef) and zillions of tiny side dishes. *Soju* (Korean whiskey) was passed around like water. All the uncles told jokes, smoked, and laughed. I had no idea what they were saying; Seong Yoon relayed much of it but was often too caught up in all the activity to remember to translate.

As we all sat on the floor, stuffing our faces with *bulgogi* and having a good time, Seong Yoon's sister decided to call their mother, whom he hadn't spoken to since he was a teenager.

"Big brother, mom is on the phone," his sister said across the table, startling all the relatives into silence.

"What did you do?" Seong Yoon asked.

"Take it, talk to her!" she demanded.

With his mouth still full of food, Seong Yoon nervously clutched the phone.

"Oma, it's your son, Seong Yoon. I'm getting married. My wife is American; you would like her."

"My son, my son," she repeated, crying on the phone.

"Come to the wedding. Just come. It would be so good to see you there," Seong Yoon pleaded.

"I can't. I'm sorry," she replied, and then wished him well before hanging up.

They haven't spoken to each other since.

While his relatives had returned to eating, drinking, and merrymaking, Seong Yoon sat quietly at the end of the table, no doubt saddened by the fact that his mother, whom he had little contact with since the divorce, refused to come to his wedding. He knew it was because she felt shame for not being part of his life. Seong Yoon felt that she wanted to keep a distance and erase the painful memories that came after his birth.

Though he'd never felt any special bond with his mother, he'd always known that something was missing from his life. Even though he received love from his grandparents, he still longed for that special kind of love that only a mother and son can share. When he was young, Seong Yoon would often have dreams of a feminine figure, much like an angel, who filled him with warmth and assured him that he was loved. Later in life, he no longer had the dream, but he still hoped he would find that same kind of warmth and love in his life. In fact, when he was a monk, there was a time when he began to see all the Buddha statues and figures around him as women.

In a letter to me once, he let me know that he had finally found in me the love that had eluded him for so long. And now that he had found it, I could understand why he didn't want to go back to the painful memories of his home life. I couldn't help wondering if we were at least in part attracted to each other because of our shared childhood experience with divorce. I too had grown up in a broken family: My parents divorced when I was five years old. While I love my family dearly and am closer to them now that I am older, there was quite a bit of tension growing up. I couldn't wait to go to college and be free. I couldn't wait to travel. I couldn't wait to find out who I was apart from my family.

Despite all of this, Seong Yoon's family had been as kind as could be. They had welcomed me into their home and had even treated me to a meal at a restaurant. I knew that where they were from, it was unusual, if not looked down upon, for a Korean man to marry a foreigner. Parts of Korea, particularly rural areas, are still quite traditional, and some parents expect their children to marry Koreans, or at least people of Korean decent. What made our wedding announcement even more unusual was the fact that a few weeks prior to our trip to Tongyeong, Seong Yoon's relatives believed he was living in the temple as a monk. I was relieved, therefore, that his relatives chose to celebrate with us, even if they didn't entirely understand or agree with what we were doing.

Two months later, the big day was fast approaching. In early May, my father and my best friend Lena flew out for the occasion. My mother didn't make the trip because she was worried about the bird flu, or at least that's the excuse I clearly remember her giving. Though when reminded of this, she now says it was the tension between North and South Korea that kept her from coming. My sister was five months pregnant at the time, so she couldn't make the trip. While I did hope that my mother and sister would be there for my wedding, I knew it was a long trip, and so I didn't have high expectations that *anyone* would make it. (We planned to have a small reception in the States that summer for friends and family.) I was quite happy in the end to have the two witnesses I had—and having just my dad and one friend made everything much more manageable, especially since there were only two extra passenger seats in our Elantra.

My dad had packed his suit and wing-tipped shoes for the occasion. I had to break the news to him that he'd be wearing something else. On the day before the wedding, the four of us ventured down the street from our high-rise apartment building to a *hanbok* rental shop. When we walked through the door, the woman working there jumped at the sight of us. I'm sure she'd clothed a fair number of wedding parties in her day, but none the likes of us.

I had already chosen my *hanbok*: a full, red skirt and a fitted white top with an embroidered circular crest on the front and blue trim around the collar and cuffs. For my dad, the shop owner selected peach silky pants that billowed out at the waist and came in tight around the ankles and a fitted blue jacket. Lena is quite tall, so it was hard to find anything long enough for her. Months before her arrival, she'd said, "I'll wear anything but bright pink." Much to her dismay, a bright pink *hanbok* was the closest one to her size. Still it was too short, revealing her ankles and a small tattoo. Seong Yoon was set to wear light pink bottoms and a blue top. We were quite the rainbow. We picked up a *hanbok* for Seong Yoon's father and one for a friend before leaving the shop and the poor exhausted shopkeeper.

The day of the wedding, we brought all of our wedding attire over to my dad's hotel. (Lena was staying with us in our apartment, where she slept on the sofa.) My dad bought us a nice buffet breakfast in the lobby, and then we went to his room to change into our clothes.

It was quite the scene. There were all kinds of interesting and confusing undergarments and overgarments to assemble. Seong Yoon was the only one who had a clue how to do any of this, so he became the dresser. He adjusted bows, tied jackets, fastened underwear, adjusted skirts, and explained the strange booty socks I had to wear with my curly-toed red shoes. We were all having fits of laughter at the sight of one another.

Fortunately, my father had already checked out, so we were able to shimmy out the door without causing too much of a scene in the lobby. But it was a different story outside. Cars slowed down to stare at us while we waited for the valet to fetch my car. After making sure that our flowing skirts and pants were all tucked in, we were off.

The wedding venue was a theme park. Not one with rollercoasters and Ferris wheels—this park was a replica of a traditional Korean village, a place where students and tourists came to learn about customs and traditions. My father was an instant celebrity there: Schoolchildren in uniforms swarmed him for autographs. I guess they'd never seen an American man wearing traditional Korean clothes at a folk village before. It was hard prying my father away from his fans, but we had to, or we'd be late to the ceremony.

We paraded all the way through the "village." We passed an ox and cart and a pseudo-farmer in a field; we walked past grass huts with people dressed in traditional clothes selling goods; we tiptoed over an ancient bridge only a foot wide. Finally, we arrived at our destination: a *yangban* (aristocrat) house, where we were to marry.

Seong Yoon's family showed up shortly after, and they all stood in a line, bowing one by one to greet my father and Lena. Fifteen or so of them—as well as many of their village neighbors—had gotten up at five in the morning and boarded a rented *norebang* (karaoke) bus to make the six-hour journey.

It was quite the sight to see my father with Seong Yoon's father. They looked like they'd switched wardrobes—my father in his peach-colored pajama pants and pointy shoes, and Seong Yoon's father in a sharp dark suit with pink suspenders and a bowtie.

Our wedding was the twelve o'clock show.

Yes, show.

Traditional wedding ceremonies were performed three times a day for the benefit of the theme-park guests. Usually, the ceremonies weren't real weddings—just performances put on by actors. But from time to time, like today, the wedding was indeed real.

But with all the fanfare and onlookers, and all the familiar people in my life doing strange things, it was hard not to feel like we were all actors in a grandiose surreal spectacle.

My father and Lena, wearing traditional Korean garb, bowed reverently to what seemed like the largest Korean family known to man. Wedding photographers by trade, a gang of black-suited uncles ran around, snapping shots like the paparazzi. As for me, I was sure I was going to faint from heatstroke what with all the clothes I was wearing. I had on two brightly colored *hanbok* (one used only for the ceremony) and a huge hairpiece that was secured in place by a two-foot-long jade hairpin. On top of the hairpiece, I wore a funky black hat (later, looking at the wedding photos, my sister aptly remarked that it looked like it was covered in gummy bears). According to custom, I was not allowed to see my husband's face until after the ceremony. With my right hand resting on top of my left, my elbows bent and a white band of silk draped over my raised forearms, I did my best to shield my face from my husband. Thank goodness I had two Korean assistants to aid me in my endless required bowing to the sun, the moon, the earth, my future husband, the relatives, and whomever else: The assistants gripped me under my armpits and lifted me up to my feet each time. My job was to keep my face covered.

I could see, out of the corner of my eye, that my father was about to cry. Twenty years ago—practically to the day—he had been in Korea for the Medical Corps. I don't think he ever imagined he'd be back in this country to watch his daughter get married to a former Buddhist monk.

After the ceremony, my husband—in his long, blue-sheathed outfit and a stovetop hat—mounted a pony. An assistant carried an enormous umbrella to shade him from the sun. I was stuffed into a *gama* (a litter, but literally meaning "emperor hauler") that was carried by four men. My heavy wedding attire weighed down on me as I sat perched on my cushion, alone within this tiny, protective space that swayed back and forth. As we paraded through the village, musicians played flutes, drums, and whistles, but it all sounded so far away from inside my box. From my little window, I watched the entire wedding party march alongside me as if I were watching a movie. My husband paraded through the village high on his pony, playing the part of nobleman quite well. He had also played the role of a son, a university student, a monk, a sushi waiter, and a yoga school owner. As of today, he had a new role to play: husband.

But looking at him then, from the window of my litter, I saw so clearly how he is so much more than any part he has ever played—how we *all* are so much more than any part we have ever played. And how the versatility with which we move from role to role proves that we are indeed greater than the sum of our parts.

Theater actor and director Constantin Stanislavsky once famously said, "There are no small parts, only small actors." But when it comes to the parts we play in this worldly drama, all roles are small in comparison to the expansive, boundless nature of a single human being.

Suffering Is the Stepping Stone to Liberation

"You desire to know the art of living, my friend?
It is contained in one phrase: make use of suffering."
—HENRI-FRÉDÉRIC AMIE

SEONG YOON had been living with me in college housing for almost a year when we learned we'd have to take in a roommate. We hadn't yet gotten married and had recently opened our yoga studio, so the timing was less than ideal. After so many years of living apart from each other, the last thing I wanted was another person sharing our space, but the college insisted.

Our new living situation was particularly trying due to clashes in lifestyles. While our roommate enjoyed many late-night bar outings with her friends, we were accustomed to getting up at the crack of dawn to open the yoga studio. Three was definitely a crowd, and the tension was palpable most of the time.

To this day I believe this roommate placement was a covert attempt by the school to get us to move out. Word had gotten out that a former monk was living with me, and I'm sure this did not go down well with my conservative boss, who I was already on the outs with for refusing to take on an additional class. So it wasn't much of a surprise when I was told, shortly after I had gotten married, that I "would not be needed" at the college at the start of the new semester in September.

By this point, I wasn't even sure I wanted to teach English, but our yoga business had only been open a little over a year, and we needed the additional income. At the time, losing my job seemed like a crisis, but as they say, when one door closes, another opens.

Instead of trying to find another job teaching English, I decided to put all my energy into the yoga business for a while. With the little money I had saved up, we leased a second space, one that could double as our apartment.

It was located in Seoul, in a new, ten-story "officetel"—a word used in Korean to denote live/work space. We had a large room with hardwood floors, a disappearing kitchen, and built-in closets, making it easy to maximize the space and to camouflage evidence that we lived there. The only furniture purchases we made were a sofa bed and a folding table and chairs.

I was to be the main teacher at the new space, because Seong Yoon was already booked with classes at our other yoga school. I was nervous about my new occupation. It was not only the first time in my life I'd be teaching yoga, but I'd also be teaching it in Korean.

"You can do it," Seong Yoon assured. "Don't think too much, just do it. It will be fine. You will do great."

I still wasn't sure though. In fact, I was seriously considering scouting out new English-teaching positions online. It would just be so much easier to fall back into what was comfortable, even if what was comfortable was far from ideal—and far from desirable.

But then Seong Yoon reminded me of something I couldn't deny: "You wanted to try something new and challenging, so here's your chance."

Put that way, there was no way I could let myself throw in the towel before I'd even tried.

My very first yoga student was a woman who lived in the office-tel. She managed to follow my broken Korean as I did my best to guide her through a series of postures. At the end of class, she smiled and said *"Gamsamnida"* (Thank you). I could tell she wanted to talk more, but we both knew that my Korean was limited.

Nonetheless, later that week, she stopped by and gave me a check for the entire month.

Slowly but surely, I started to get students from the surrounding office buildings—some of whom spoke English, making it a bit easier on me.

Within a few months, I had about ten regular students, which was about all the space could handle anyway. (The space was much smaller than our other school, which could easily hold about thirty.) To add to his student numbers, Seong Yoon got into contact with an American School teacher who was looking for an English-speaking yoga class. Before we knew it, we had two extra classes set up to accommodate over fifteen American teachers.

Just when things didn't seem like they could get any better, a Korean psychologist I used to teach English to contacted me. She was involved in a TV documentary produced by SBS TV, and they wanted to interview her about ways of overcoming stress. She had been one of the first yoga students back when Seong Yoon taught in the living room of my college apartment. While she hadn't been to a class since we opened our new schools, she remembered how good she felt as a result of the yoga.

"Kathy, would Seong Yoon be interested in being interviewed by SBS TV for a documentary on stress?" she asked.

"I think he'd be thrilled!" I exclaimed.

"Okay. I'll give your contact information to the producers, and they'll be in touch with him."

Within a few weeks, Seong Yoon had set up a date and time to be interviewed. The news team wanted to come to the suburban school to film part of a class, and to interview Seong Yoon and a few students.

I was so excited. On the day of the interview, I had to teach a yoga class from five to six, and the reporter and film crew planned to be at the yoga school by seven—giving me just enough time to get there to watch. As soon as I finished my class and ushered my students out the door, I opened the closet, grabbed a dress, and pulled it over my head. I slipped on some tights, dabbed on a bit of makeup, put on my boots and jacket, and headed out the door to the subway. On the way there, all I could think about was how famous our studio was going to be.

I almost missed my stop because of my daydreams. Riding the escalator up to the ticket area, and walking the remaining steps out of the subway into the fall air, I almost skipped down the street. OM SHANTI YOGA CENTER read our giant sign, a beacon of light among all the other neon signs, which were advertising bars, billiards, and fried chicken. I rushed up the stairs to the fourth floor and burst through the door, ready to greet the camera people.

"Hi, how are you?" said Seong Yoon, sitting all alone on the floor of the studio.

"Where's SBS? Where's the reporter? What happened to the program about stress?"

"They were here. You missed them. They came earlier, while you were in class. I wanted to let you know, but I knew you'd be teaching yoga, and I didn't want to disturb you."

I pulled off my boots and plunked myself down onto the floor next to Seong Yoon.

"I can't believe I missed them. This was our moment, and I missed it."

"You didn't miss it. You were teaching yoga, and that's why they came. They came because we are offering something wonderful here. Don't worry. You are my other half, so half of you was in that interview," he said.

"So how was it?"

"Well, they came in with their cameras and filmed a bit of the class. Afterward, they interviewed a few students, and then they interviewed me. It was good."

"What did you say?"

"You'll see it Friday night, when they air it. They'll send us a copy of the tape too."

"But we are teaching yoga on Friday."

"Well, they promised to send us the tape within a week of broadcasting the documentary, so we'll see it soon enough."

The following Saturday, Seong Yoon and I slept in; weekends were happily class free. We were so hungry that we decided to go down the street for a sandwich. The cashier instantly recognized Seong Yoon.

"Hey, I saw you on TV last night!" he said. And then the two of them broke into a full discussion. There was a lot of laughing and smiling happening, but I didn't really follow the conversation.

"He said the show was amazing," Seong Yoon translated.

"Now I really want to see it!" I said, smiling at the cashier.

When the tape arrived the next week, we snuggled up together on the couch with some snacks in preparation for "the viewing."

It opened with a woman boarding a bus with an axe in hand. She was so stressed out that she threatened to chop up the bus driver. It continued by showing people losing it here and there in one way or another. Faces were fuzzed out on the screen, and voices were morphed into a robotic sound to protect identities. The subjects continued to talk about all the stress they had; the terrible things they had done to themselves and to their families and friends; and what medications they were taking to alleviate some of their copious stress.

To be honest, the program wasn't very inspiring. Most of it was downright depressing, in fact.

But then Seong Yoon appeared. Candles flickered in the background as yoga students moved with ease in and out of postures. Seong Yoon came on at the very end and was asked why people practice yoga.

"When people come here, they aren't always in good condition. They have a lot of stress, and they are looking for something to relieve that stress. Recognizing that you are stressed is the first step in freeing yourself from it." He concluded by saying, "Practice yoga, and everything will be okay." Then they cut to a close-up of his glowing face, followed by a shot of a group of youngsters running down the street, holding hands and giggling.

From axe-wielding bus passenger to happy, laughing children—all in a half hour. Now that's good television!

Needless to say, business picked up shortly after the program aired. And with our two schools thriving, I decided it was safe to take some time off. We had been working full-time for almost a year and needed a break. I planned to go to the States to attend a thirty-day silent meditation course, and Lena was getting married. How could I miss it? After all, she had trudged all the way to Korea for my wedding, even agreeing to wear a bright pink puffy Korean *hanbok* against her will. There was no way I was missing her wedding, even if I had to swim to the States. (She'd asked that Seong Yoon perform a Buddhist ritual for the wedding, so he'd be joining me in the States for a few weeks, too.)

Of course, we needed to find replacement teachers. Our friend Jeremy from Long Island agreed to take a break from his teaching gig to come take over my classes at the officetel, and a few Korean teachers would cover Seong Yoon's classes.

Lena's wedding day was Seattle's hottest day of the year, and it took place on a steamboat on Lake Union. The boat captain was to officiate, but before then, Seong Yoon—who had to brush up on his *moktak* skills in record time—chanted sutras in Korean. We listened patiently at first, even though we were all dripping in sweat. But just as it sounded like his chant might end, he continued on for another verse. And another one, and another one—to the dismay of the entire wedding party, I'm sure. It sounded lovely, but these two were ready to get married, and we were all ready to get out of the hot sun.

I finally elbowed him on the tenth verse, and he wrapped it up. He'd shut his eyes, so maybe he'd forgotten where he was—maybe he thought he was back in the temple. I bet he never thought he'd be performing his sacred chants as a wedding number on an old steamboat on Lake Union in Seattle.

Our time in the States passed quickly. Before I knew it, Seong Yoon was headed back to Korea to hold down the yoga fort, and I was headed to Massachusetts for a thirty-day meditation retreat.

After reading about my first experience on that ten-day course in Nepal, you may wonder why I ever wanted to subject myself to a course that was three times as long. It's true: that first experience was definitely a trial for me, and after it was over, I vowed to Seong Yoon that I'd never step foot inside a Vipassana retreat again. The suffering was too unbearable. I even remember using the words "pure torture." And yet, ever since, I continued to participate in meditation retreats—at least once a year, sometimes more.

"Why?" you may ask. "What are you, a glutton for punishment?"

To be honest, I have no idea. Every time I arrive at a new retreat, I wonder how I ended up there. And each time, despite all the work I've done in previous courses, the pain, the suffering, and the mental challenges are all waiting there for me. I just pick up right where I left off.

So yes: Doing a retreat that would last three times longer than usual was daunting. In fact, during the first part of the orientation, all I could think was, *Thirty days, thirty days, thirty days.* But then the administration made an announcement that distracted me from my unhelpful mental chanting: Construction would be taking place on the grounds during the retreat.

It wasn't the first time I'd heard this news. I had been warned about the construction in the literature I received upon my acceptance to the course, but I didn't think it would be a problem. After all, I was a seasoned meditator. I could get through these distractions. This reminder and the reality of the impending course, however, put me in a state of unease.

We were assured we'd be removed from the action, that it would not cause too much of a disturbance. Not removed enough apparently. Inches from my cabin, workers tore down a barn as they swore and swapped sex stories. Being that we had no outside stimulus and were in silence, these conversations added some unwanted food for thought. During the afternoons, in my meditation cell, the ground would shake from constant drilling. I was so sensitive by this point, I felt like the drilling was going on in my cell.

The meditation teacher—perhaps realizing that we might all be about to self-combust—called us all in one by one to check in with us.

"Are you feeling any mental agitation?" she asked.

"Well, I think I'm doing okay, but it does feel like the drilling is happening in my cell, and the destruction of the barn was a rude awakening," I said. (Not to mention the workers, who got me thinking about sex. But I chose to keep that bit to myself.)

"Good. Well, just continue with the practice, and if you have any questions or concerns, you can always meet me."

A few days later, there was a note on my door.

Please secure all of your belongings or anything that might be loose and could roll around. Your cabin will be moved to the women's walking area tomorrow at 3:30 PM.

Moved? How exactly do you move a cabin, and why? Sure enough, at 3:30 sharp, as I exited my meditation cell, I watched as a forklift cruised down the service road with my cabin, leaving me in a cloud of dust. Now I was not only speechless, I was homeless. I went back to my cell and meditated a bit more, trying not to focus on the fact that my house was gone. When I came out of my cell for tea-time, I located my house in the women's walking area, in the grass, close to a tree. The steps had crumbled after the forklift dumped it, so I had to climb up to my front door from then on. In addition to the broken steps, the door was jammed shut from the impact, and I had to go to the dining hall, get a knife, and pry my way in. After that, I always left my door slightly open for fear of being locked out.

But now, with the construction workers gone, I was less distracted and more able to focus my attention inward. And by day twenty, I felt I had become meditation itself. It seemed effortless. Whether I was eating, walking, sleeping, or sitting, I was in the practice. I could not distinguish the parameters of myself anymore. I was an empty vessel. I was boundless.

It is not unusual for images and sensations to arise and pass in deep meditation. So slowly, as the debris was weeded from my mind, memories accompanied by sensations began to arise in my mind and body. Some were pleasant, some unpleasant, and some neutral. But no matter the sensation, I tried not to hold onto or chase these memories; the point was to stay with the practice and just observe them. Through observing them without attachment, they passed.

I soldiered on, and before I knew it, I had meditated for thirty days.

The beginning of the course was definitely challenging, and I experienced quite a bit of mental agitation: annoyance at the construction, physical pain, food cravings, songs stuck in my head, drowsiness, boredom, and loneliness. But I had participated in enough courses by this time to know that these were part of the deal, and that they would all come to pass eventually.

The last half of the course flew by. I was in a rhythm. I was practicing the meditation, and my every action, thought, and emotion dissolved into that practice. Still, by the time I had reached the end of the course, I couldn't believe I had survived.

It was the meditation itself that got me through. As long as I stayed with the practice, stayed in the now, I was just fine. The only requirement was to keep on going, through whatever came my way.

There will always be suffering, but Buddhism teaches us that if we can just bear witness to the suffering instead of attaching to it, it will subside, and eventually, we will be free from it. It is not that suffering will no longer exist—it is that we will no longer be attached to it. Suffering can come in the form of pain or even pleasure. Food, for example, would occasionally float past me in my cell. It was usually all the food I was missing: chocolate, sushi, a flakey croissant with almond paste alongside a perfect-foam cappuccino. (What can I say? I'm a Seattle girl.) I could practically taste them all. But I came to realize early on in my practice that whenever I wanted something that was not there, it was a cause of suffering for me . . . and I'm not only talking about food here.

This realization was so tremendous for me. It changed my entire way of viewing and living my life. And it would especially come in handy soon after my return to Korea.

I suppose you can't just walk away from your life for three months and expect everything to be the same when you return.

And it wasn't. Almost all of my students had left, or at least taken a break. Many knew I'd be out of town, but I guess the news didn't really sink in until the day my substitute—Jeremy, a hairy Long Islander who liked to do yoga by sweating it out shirtless—took over. Without a doubt, this scared away my timid and modest Korean yoginis—they were shy enough wearing stretch pants. Shirtless in Korea was not the done thing. People kept their shirts on even when it was a hundred degrees outside. In fact, showing any kind of skin was considered a little risqué, unless you were on a beach.

Of course, I was still thankful Jeremy agreed to step in and take over my classes. Otherwise I wouldn't have been able to go to Lena's wedding or attend the meditation retreat. But since student numbers had dropped, I had to teach private English classes on the side to make ends meet.

Somehow we managed to keep both schools going, and by winter, they bounced back. Since we were on track again, Seong Yoon decided to attend a ten-day meditation course in Japan, and I filled in for him while he was gone.

Boy, was he surprised to discover the turn of events that had occurred at our suburban studio during the short time he was away. During *savasana*—the resting portion of the yoga class—the floor started vibrating, and you could hear the sound of a thousand pounding hooves. Then it came. An announcer shouted, *"Sam, sam, sa, sa!"* ("Three, three, four, four!") Seong Yoon turned up the flute music to try to muffle out the ruckus going on below us. Yoga students, laying flat on their backs under fleece blankets, opened their eyes a peek, curious as to what was happening. They couldn't help but start to chuckle. Apparently, horseracing had moved in downstairs.

Koreans sat around all day below the studio, betting on the ponies on a large movie screen. Since gambling was technically illegal, the exchange of cash took place in a truck in the back parking lot.

Our school went from being an oasis of peace to being smack-dab in the middle of a full-on gambling operation.

This would not do. Seong Yoon put his foot down and demanded his deposit back.

Within the month, we had moved down the street to a more expensive place—a second-floor studio in a four-story building next to an acupuncture clinic. Above us was a health club, and on the top floor was a fundamentalist church. For the most part, it was quiet, but every now and then you'd hear dumbbells crashing to the floor. Still, we'd take it over horseracing in a heartbeat. And as long as the holy rollers restricted their shouting and praising to the fourth floor, we'd be okay.

The question was whether we could afford it. It was a huge jump in price, and just because it was nicer didn't necessarily mean more people would attend. We had already attracted all the yoga-minded people from this traditional neighborhood. We had exhausted our resources in this suburban town.

Our downtown location was great, but the student numbers had dwindled since my visit overseas, so we had to give it up in March. This also meant that we had to give up our home. And there was no way the two of us could live in the new yoga school in the suburbs being that it lacked everything needed to "live."

A new English teaching gig at a university not only would provide a guaranteed income, it would also give us a home, so I touched up my resume, sent it out, and got another job. But not in the city: No, this job was practically in North Korea. No joke. It was only twenty miles from the border, far away from our yoga school. There was no way Seong Yoon would be able to commute, so we had to move away from each other.

This just about killed me. Again? I mean, come on. We were married now. Shouldn't we finally be able to be together? It had taken so much for us to get to this point. We'd been over the highest mountain pass in the world, forged a river that swelled so high I thought it would be the end of one of us, suffered through dysentery and theft in India, endured a forbidden relationship for years, and lived off of pocket change on many occasions. Clearly, I had proven that I was willing to do whatever it took.

But this? You want me to move to North Korea, practically?

I thought I was done with suffering in this relationship. I thought I was home free now.

But I was wrong. Just because I'd made it to this point didn't mean it was over. My meditation had surely taught me that. No, the suffering was not over, but the only way through it, I had learned through my practice, was to face it. I knew that when I ran away from the things that gave me pain, I only had more pain.

As much as I knew this, it was still hard to accept the situation. Liberation from suffering was still out there on the distant horizon, as much as I had taken baby steps toward it. I wasn't immune to pain, and I still fought and agonized and pleaded in a futile effort to rid myself of it.

The school I taught at was like a prison on the top of a cliff. Every day—in my old blue Elantra with a shot transmission—I'd zigzag my way up a mountain, between rice fields, past farmers, on my way to the school. My boss was a very stern woman who had a tight grip on her "girls," the students attending the isolated school.

When I expressed concern that they were so cut off from society at the prime of their lives, I was told it was good for them; they could focus more on their studies if they didn't have any distractions.

It seemed wrong to me. And was I aiding and abetting this by teaching there? The whole situation made me feel miserable.

Seong Yoon wasn't exactly living the high life either. He ended up living in the studio, which, as I mentioned, was not equipped for living. He had no shower or kitchen. To bathe, he squatted down in the bathroom with a hole for a toilet, turned on a hose by the sink, filled a bucket with cold water, and dumped it over his head. Then he'd soap himself down while shivering, and dump another bucket over his head to rinse off. He ate a lot of takeout and slept on an old foldout sofa in the lobby of the school. I only saw him on weekends, when he made the long bus ride north to stay with me.

We had been enduring this situation for almost six months when I called him one evening, crying.

"I can't understand why I have to live here," I sobbed.

"What can we do? We don't have money. At least you have a job," he said.

"I know, but I'd rather be poor and be with you. I don't think I can take it much longer!"

I felt isolated, alone, and miserable. Again.

At night, drunken Koreans sat right below my window at an open-air bar, finishing off little green bottles of *soju* until all hours of the night. They would yell and scream and eventually pass out. I didn't sleep much. I cried a lot. I felt like I had been sent to prison. The only thing that saved me were the innocent, smiling faces of my students during the week, and my weekends with Seong Yoon.

When he came to visit he put me at ease. We even ventured out past military checkpoints to several hot-spring areas and a national park. The land was so untouched, so rugged and primitive out there. For a country that is so overpopulated, it was surprising to find ourselves completely alone while camping out on big boulders with a pristine river below us. We'd walk naked out on the rocks and swim with the green frogs in the pools. There, I felt like I was at the end of the earth and, temporarily, the end of suffering.

But I wasn't. Suffering continued as soon as I came back to the work week. *Do I really have to suffer through all this again?* I lamented. *What am I learning from living out here all alone?*

I didn't see it then, but now I realize what it was.

By suffering through this time, I was learning what I *didn't* want in my life. It ended up taking me a long time to realize it, that's for sure. For years, out of fear, I had fallen back, again and again, into what I knew, but that didn't make it a comfortable existence. I was not in this world to simply "exist." I had dreams. I had goals.

I wanted to write. I dreamed of living in a nice little house with my husband. I imagined a place with a yard, a colorful garden, and all the appropriate living spaces—somewhere peaceful and quiet, yet close enough to all the action. Somewhere, perhaps *not* in Korea even. I was ready for that life—I wanted that life. I knew that suffering was part of life, but I hoped it would include a few other things, too. You know, like peace, joy, and a sense of purpose. And I was sure those things were out there (or in there) because I'd had them in my life before.

I just had to find them again.

Honor Your Past

What you are is what you have been.
What you'll be is what you do now.
—THE BUDDHA

SOMETIMES IT TAKES a fresh face to put things in perspective, to see things for how they really are, and to get things back on track.

In my case, that fresh face was my mother.

She came to visit me in Korea. It was a spontaneous decision and I'm still not really sure what prompted her to come. Obviously she wanted to see me, but why then? Why almost three years *after* my wedding in Korea? But she's always been like that. Her reasons for doing or not doing things have always eluded me. As much as this annoys me, it's also part of her allure. She has a way of convincing me that something is a "great idea," like the time she talked me into abandoning my job at the health club and traveling with her across the United States for four months.

Before I knew what hit me, we'd both quit our jobs, and friends and family gathered around for a send-off. I still can't believe I agreed to go on a 15,000-mile journey across America in very cramped quarters with my mother. Was I nuts?

Perhaps.

So who knows what crazy hair caused her to fly across the Pacific to South Korea. Perhaps she regretted missing my wedding (we ended up visiting the wedding location during her trip), or maybe she was there to convince me that "home" was a pretty good place to settle down.

I'll never forget her reaction when she saw where and how I was living. On the way to the college where I was teaching, my car, with its bad transmission, hopped its way up the hill with jerky stops and starts. She was shocked—not only at how my car was operating, but at where we were.

"How the hell did you find this place, Kathy?"

The frightened look on her face made me realize how far off the map I'd gone. Here I was, living pretty much off the grid—in the middle of nowhere, Korea—with a broken-down car, far away from my husband.

Now, all the questions I'd been asking myself, again and again— *Did I choose this life? What happened to me?*—were answered by her horrified expression.

"Just come home," she said.

Come home?

Now there was an idea I hadn't thought about in awhile—not since I tried to convince Seong Yoon to stay with me in America before we were even married. The truth is, I had a love/hate relationship with the "home" my mother spoke of. I'd spent much of my adult life trying to leave "home" and my past behind me.

But deep down, my mother's suggestion hit a nerve. I'd lived in Korea long enough, and as much as I loved it and still love it, it was time to go.

Living in the United States, after living almost ten years in Asia, would not be easy. Where would we stay? What would we do? How would we survive? I knew I wouldn't be able to handle living with my parents and working at the coffee shop down the street again. I still had my dignity, after all.

For some reason, my mother didn't think this was such a big problem. "Just get on a plane and come home," she said. "The rest will work itself out."

After discussing my plan with Seong Yoon, he agreed to give it a try—partly because he knew it would make me happy and also because he was excited about the new adventure. He had exhausted all his resources at his yoga school in the suburbs and he wasn't getting many new students. Now, at least, he had job experience he could use in the States. So we made a plan to move to the States after my one-year teaching contract was up in February.

In the meantime, we were able to get some time off together in the summer to travel to Hong Kong for a meditation course. The Hong Kong Vipassana organization had yet to establish a permanent meditation center, so the course took place at a rented site in the New Territories, way out in the sticks, in a swampy area dotted with makeshift buildings. Mosquitoes buzzed all over the place. I wondered how we would make it through ten days in such primitive environs.

I was expecting a teacher from Hong Kong, but when I got there, I read that he was American. His name looked familiar, but I couldn't place where I knew it from.

"You went to the University of Puget Sound?" he said incredulously as he meandered toward me, wearing sandals, socks, slacks, and a long shirt—no doubt to protect him from the mosquito infestation.

"Yes, I did."

"How did you get all the way out here?" he asked.

"Good question," I said, wondering the same about him.

"I'm the area teacher in Washington State."

Ah-ha! Now it was all coming back to me.

Years ago, during many of my breaks from teaching in Korea, I'd spent time at the meditation center in Washington State. At the end of a three-day course I took back in 2000, the teacher called me upstairs to her living quarters. I couldn't fathom why: Teachers only met with students if there was a problem; they didn't call them up to their rooms just to chat.

"So, I wanted to talk to you about something," she said. "We are looking for center managers. We would be able to provide a house for you and your husband. Would you be interested?"

My husband? A house? Whoa, Nellie. Let's slow this boat down. First of all, Seong Yoon and I were on the outs—that was during our roller-coaster phase. Second of all, I was returning to Asia, I had a job to get back to. I had promises to keep.

"Um, I'm not married, and I live in Asia right now, but I'll keep it in mind for the future," I replied.

"Well, think about it, and if you are interested, you can contact David Thatcher," she said.

And who should be standing in front of me, six years later, in this bug-infested camp in Hong Kong, but David Thatcher himself.

"Are you currently looking for center managers? Because we are planning on moving back to Washington in February," I asked, full of optimism.

"Not currently," he said. "But we'll keep it mind for the future."

For a few moments, I allowed myself to hope that the future David Thatcher spoke of might be sooner rather than later, but decided to let that thought go and focus on the course—which was more like a test of survival. If we weren't eaten alive by mosquitoes in the afternoon, the bedbugs were sure to finish us off at night. And apparently, I didn't get the memo about bringing my own plate and silverware. I arrived at the mess hall on the first day and found food, but nothing to eat it with. Everyone else had nice little compartmentalized plastic containers and cases containing their eating utensils. With a bit of sign language (imaginary fork scooping food into mouth), I managed to get across to the cook that I was chopstick-less in Hong Kong. She shuffled around under the sink, clamoring pots and pans, surely startling the poor, silent participants on the course. Finally she emerged—glasses askew, hair amiss—with plastic chopsticks and a plastic bowl smaller than the ones monks use for begging. But hey, at least I wouldn't starve. I wondered how Seong Yoon was faring on the men's side. Did he also have to resort to sign language for survival purposes?

On the last day of the course, when we came out of silence, I met Seong Yoon. He hadn't lost too much weight, so I figured he'd sorted out the food-eating predicament. But the mosquitoes had left him itching to get out the place in more ways than one. We said our farewell to the teacher, and he said he'd pass our email addresses on to the center's management committee back in Washington.

We sold our yoga business, I quit my job, and all that remained was for us pack up our lives into one suitcase each and move out of my college-housing apartment. We did our best to get rid of everything we could, and mailed boxes back to the States packed with things we simply couldn't part with. On our last day, a Korean teacher from the college stopped in to do a walkthrough. Our two suitcases were already on the front step.

"Everything looks good," she said.

"Great," I replied. We stepped out of the apartment, and I handed her the keys. She locked up, wished us luck, and left.

We dragged our suitcases down two flights of stairs and into the snow. It was teeth-clatteringly cold, and the wind felt like it was cutting through my skin. Seong Yoon hailed a cab, and we rode twenty minutes to an airport-bus stop in the middle of nowhere. There wasn't a car or a person to be found. The wind howled across the desolate landscape and bit at our faces; the wheels of our suitcases sank in the snow. Suddenly, Korea felt as foreign to me as the day I first arrived—the difference was that Seong Yoon, my husband, was holding my gloved hand, tightly.

"Are you sure we're in the right place?" I asked, covering my face with my scarf.

"I hope so," he said.

Thirty minutes later, a speck appeared in the distance. Thank god. I was frozen. Once on the warm bus, I let go. We were on our way, and there was no going back now.

So much had happened in Asia. I came there with the intention of staying a year—two, maximum. Now, here I was, over ten years later, finally leaving Asia for good . . . and married to a monk.

Korea had certainly left her mark on me, and I would never be the same. I'd shed a river of tears on her dry soil. I'd learned to love sitting on her *ondol* floors in the winter, eating noodle soup with chopsticks. And I'd miss her many teashops—especially the one where I realized the bald man sitting across from me was my husband-to-be.

My mother and stepfather were waiting for us at the airport in Seattle. Luckily, a month before we arrived, my stepfather's tenant had moved out of his rental house after eleven years. So we now had a place to stay. But it was in dire need of repair. So before we arrived, my mom and stepdad rolled up their sleeves and set out to bring the house back to life. She called it their "Habitat for Humanity project."

Once we arrived, we put a lot of time and effort into the house as well. To the amazement of the neighbors, Seong Yoon single-handedly painted the entire house in one day. Many of them watched in awe as my limber monk–turned–yoga-teacher husband balanced himself on a ladder, roller in one hand and paint bucket in the other. They cheered when he got down to his last square foot of house. A woman walking her dog couldn't believe she was looking at the same house.

"It was a terrible pastel blue when I walked my dog this morning! Now look at it. Gorgeous!" she exclaimed.

At least we were off to a good start with the neighbors.

While we were in the middle of faux-painting the kitchen mustard yellow, our boxes arrived from Korea. Inside them were photo albums, paintings, clothes, little treasures from Korea, books—all of the possessions that had meaning in our lives. Even though we were moving on to a new chapter of our lives together, we weren't willing to completely forget the past. After all, the past is what got us here in the first place. Remembering what we had been through together gave us the strength to move ahead.

Many of those who follow Buddhism believe that by purging yourself of possessions, you are practicing detachment. I've even heard of people so determined to leave their past behind that they take all reminders of their life before, gather them into a giant pile, and set it aflame. I, myself, had thought that by leaving my home and traveling, I could leave my past behind and start a new life. But I'd finally learned that this is not how it works. I carried my past with me to every new country I visited or lived in, gathering new experiences to add to the pile. Those new experiences did not replace my past; instead, they helped me see it in a new light.

It hadn't been easy for me and Seong Yoon to leave Korea behind. But as we cruised up and down the main strip by our house, it looked like Korea had followed us. Right around the corner, at a Korean grocery store, we could buy homemade kimchi, and across the street from there was a great place for *bibimbap*—a delicious spicy mix of rice, meat, and vegetables.

And it wasn't just the housing and food situation that had panned out so easily for us—we soon learned that we both had jobs!

While we were fixing up the house, we got a call from the management committee at the Vipassana center in Washington. They needed center managers to fill in during the summer and wondered if we could both start training for that position in April. The timing couldn't have been more perfect too: We wouldn't have been able to start earlier, as we'd planned to go to Massachusetts in late February to participate in a thirty-day silent meditation course.

We decided to keep our house in Seattle while we lived at the center in the summer. The small stipend we made as center managers was just enough to pay our rent for the house, and at the center, there were no expenses for food or lodging. Our job was to buy all the food, pick students up from train and bus stops, troubleshoot, orient the students and kitchen staff at the beginning of every ten-day course, take care of all office work, and generally make sure that the courses ran smoothly. These ten-day courses ran continuously, so there was a lot to manage. Managing any business is hard, but it helped that we were required to meditate two hours a day, minimum. All hell could have broken loose, but in that kind of environment, anything seemed manageable.

By the end of the summer though, I started to get a bit worried. We'd be returning to our house without jobs. Before we knew we'd be working at the meditation center for the summer, I'd tried to secure a teaching position at a local community college. Later, I learned that most of the community colleges in the area required that their teachers at least have a master's degree. I was sure there were hundreds of qualified applicants for these jobs, and that my resume was either tossed out immediately or at the bottom of a slush pile. So I gave up on that idea completely. I figured I could work at a department store or something. It was kind of depressing to imagine working in retail after spending over a decade as a teacher.

I'm not sure why I still didn't fully trust the universe. So many things had worked out—what was different with this situation?

One day that summer at the center, after a ten-day course had ended, I was up in the meditation teacher's room, going over some paperwork, when she turned to me and said, "What will you do for a job after the summer is over?"

"I don't know," I said, not happy to be reminded of the situation.

"Well, what was your job before?" she asked.

"I was an ESL teacher for over ten years."

"Do you know Steve Parker? He's a meditation teacher, and he's worked as an ESL teacher in the community colleges for twenty years," she said.

A few weeks later I met Steve at the center.

"So, I hear you're looking for a job," he said, smiling.

"Yes," I replied.

"Well, let's see what we can do."

A week or so after we returned to Seattle, I received a call.

I went in for an interview at a community college twenty minutes from my house. However, it wasn't really an interview. Apparently, they had already decided—because of a recommendation from Steve—that they would hire me. I had a job. In the fall, I would teach two classes—composition, and speaking and listening—to international students. And with the connections we made at the meditation center, Seong Yoon had set up several yoga classes in our living room within weeks of returning to Seattle. Things were starting to come together.

The meditation center wanted us back in the winter, and asked us to commit for an entire year. Our experience serving there had been so rewarding that we decided to do it. It was a risk, but by then, we were pretty used to risks, and I was beginning to believe that things really would work out for the best. We rented out our house, and at the end of my first quarter on the job, I let the community college know that I'd be taking a year off, but that I would love to return.

Near the end of that year at the center, I applied for a fifteen-day Teacher's Self Course in India with S. N. Goenka, the man who founded Vipassana centers internationally. Since the price to India was steep for two people, Seong Yoon decided to stay behind. I was accepted into the course, but I considered canceling. It just didn't seem right to travel there without Seong Yoon.

Much to our surprise, weeks later, he received an email letting him know that he had been accepted into the course.

The baffling part was that *he never even applied*. This was unheard of. Getting accepted to this particular course was tough. It required a recommendation from a teacher and a lengthy application. No one knew how he got in. I called it "divine intervention"—he was meant to be there. How could he refuse to go after he had been mysteriously accepted?

But this still didn't solve our money situation, so we decided to forego the trip. Just as we had given up, a local meditation teacher heard about our plight and Seong Yoon's amazing story and decided to loan us the money to fly to India.

So eleven years later, we found ourselves back in familiar territory. Everything was coming full circle, and we felt so fortunate to be able to honor our past together. Being in this part of the world brought back many memories. It was on top of one of the highest mountain passes in the world, in the neighboring country of Nepal, that I first heard of Vipassana. That first course was one of the hardest things I'd ever done, and traveling in India was also challenging. I got sick, we lost our money, and we almost lost our minds from all the chaos. At the time, I vowed never to set foot on the grounds of another meditation course again. Or in India for that matter. But now, looking back on that trying time, I see how important it was to my present life—how it was then that seeds were sown for the bounty that I reap today. So much had changed: Here I was, more than a decade later, a seasoned traveler and a regular meditator. And our second trip to India was nothing like the first. First of all, we weren't cursed with so many problems, and secondly, India— particularly the meditation center—seemed magical. I wondered if this was due to the space Seong Yoon and I were now in, personally. I wondered if India was different because we were different. And I wondered if we were different at least in part because of how India had changed us the first time.

In the early morning of the first day, a sea of people in colorful saris and sandals headed to the pagoda for meditation. As I climbed the stairs from my residence, the smell of plumeria wafted through the air around me. I took off my shoes at the entrance of the pagoda and felt the cool cement on my bare feet.

In the silence of my cell, in the wee hours of the morning, I heard the clinking of the wind chimes on top of the pagoda, a yogi chanting in the valley below, and then nothing but the beat of my heart. I was back again, in my rose-colored *shalwar kameez*—the one that Seong Yoon bought for me many years ago, not far from where we were now. While I sat quietly in my cell, with eyes closed and legs folded, I was comforted by the fact that hundreds of other meditators were doing the same. I didn't feel difficulty or pain. Instead, I felt tremendous gratitude.

After our return from India, we settled back into our house in Seattle. Fortunately, I was able to get back my teaching job at the college, and Seong Yoon picked up a few yoga classes.

One day, while rummaging around in the basement, I came across an unopened box from Korea. I ripped it opened and found a piece of Seong Yoon's past that he wasn't willing to part with. It was wrapped in a beautiful piece of bright orange silk.

"Look at this," I said to Seong Yoon, who was busy organizing all the junk we had already accumulated. He left his task and came to my side to see what treasure I had found. With Seong Yoon looking over my shoulder, I carefully untied the silk. Inside was his gray monk robe and pants. They had been washed, starched, and pressed. They looked brand new.

"Are these in case you decide to join the temple again?" I joked. He smiled and gathered up the bundle to place in a container in the basement.

They are currently enshrined there, in honor of his past.

Afterword

THERE'S SOMETHING I didn't tell you.

When I attended that first thirty-day meditation retreat you read about in Lesson Nine, something strange happened. On day twenty-two, I was sitting in my cell meditating, feeling my breath and my natural body sensations, when I saw the image of a book. I also saw the title, the pages, and the chapters. It was as if someone had placed it in front of me, opened it, and slowly flipped all the pages right in front of my eyes.

I shook off this image and continued with my practice. But from that day to the end of the course, the book kept coming back. At first I was irritated by the image, because it felt like a distraction. But finally, realizing I had no control over it, I surrendered. I allowed it to be.

The title of the book was *Lessons from the Monk I Married.*

Yes, this very book you are holding in your hands.

It still sends shivers up my spine to remember this experience—even now, as I sit here writing in the low light of my office, late at night on December 20, 2010. It's now been a little over six years since I first saw this book in my mind's eye. It was slow in coming to fruition, and perhaps a lot of that had to do with the fact that I didn't really believe what I saw. I also didn't understand why or how this book would be written. In fact, I often wonder whether I *did* write it, as odd as that sounds.

The book, as it turned out, started as a blog of the same name. But in the blog, I steered away from telling the story of my relationship with Seong Yoon, preferring to leave that for this book. Instead, the blog focused on 365 lessons, one for each day of 2010.

Within five months, I watched the blog go from a few hundred readers to over 10,000. At the time of writing this, over 36,000 readers from over a hundred different countries have visited. I've received hundreds of comments, personal letters, and requests for preordered copies of this book. I've also made personal connections and close friends as a result of the blog.

One day, a writer in Montana who found my blog got in touch with me. Reading her message, I discovered she had just published a book and was about to go on tour. She said she wanted to help fellow writers, since she struggled for over a decade to get published. (Incidentally, her book went on to hit No. 18 on the *New York Times* bestseller list within weeks of it being published.)

We ended up talking to each other for an hour by phone. By the end of our conversation, I made the decision to send my proposal to this writer's agent, and she, in turn, contacted her agent to let her know we had spoken. Within a week of sending my proposal to this agent, I received representation for this book you are reading right now.

I only sent my book to one agent. I know that this is not the norm, but perhaps the time was ripe for my story to be told. I had no idea how to go about getting a book published when I started. I have been a writer all my life. I have closets full of journals, but I never thought I'd share my thoughts with the public. Writing for me was always personal. It was my therapy. It had saved me during so many periods of my life that were challenging. It had become a dear friend to me, a private friend.

Not until I first started my blog in 2009 did I realize that others could relate to my feelings and emotions, and that perhaps there was something universal to what I was feeling and experiencing.

I am so amazed at the response so far to what I have written. When I expressed this amazement to my husband, he simply said, "What people need most in life these days is inspiration, and that is what you are offering through your writing."

And in turn, it has been Seong Yoon who has offered me so much inspiration. It has been truly awe-inspiring to witness how he has thrived in the United States. Considering the fact that when he arrived, he knew only my family and a few close friends, it has been amazing to watch his business grow from a few students in our living room to a full-fledged yoga studio. His students love him and instantly know that there is something very different and special about their teacher. No one can help but be touched and inspired by him.

And the name of his school would come to him from a chance encounter with someone he felt akin to—someone he was sure was his brother in a past life.

One day, several years ago, Seong Yoon was reading a book at the Seattle public library, when, out of the corner of his eye, he spied a Tibetan monk across the room, browsing. When he approached him, the monk knew right away that Seong Yoon had also been a monk at one time. It seemed as if they had known each other for a very long time. They became fast friends. The monk's name was Sonam Rinpoche, and he is recognized by the Dalai Lama himself.

My husband took this Rinpoche, with his flowing robes in mustard and saffron, on a walk around Green Lake. It must have been a sight to behold: two Asian men, one robed and bald, the other in yoga pants and a T-shirt (and also bald; monk life will always be a part of Seong Yoon). After their walk, my husband took the Rinpoche to Starbucks for a hot cocoa.

It is not easy to have the undivided attention of this Rinpoche, but we were fortunate enough to listen to him chant in our house, take a forest hike with him, eat lunch together, and listen to him speak about happiness and compassion to a large group in our living room.

While taking a walk with Seong Yoon one day, the Rinpoche suddenly announced, "You are yoga bliss."

My husband took that very seriously.

At the time, he was keen on opening a large yoga studio in Seattle, hoping it would benefit hundreds of people. The problem was, we still didn't have much money. When I expressed my doubts over the possibility, he said, "Someone will appear and invest in this idea." I imagined a man in a flashy suit with sparkling white teeth and a fancy sports car suddenly appearing in our lives. After all, it had to be someone with money.

That's not how it happened though. Weeks later, a humble friend who was wondering what he was meant to do with his life contacted Seong Yoon. After a long talk, he decided he wanted to invest in the business. The school—which is now thriving and benefiting so many people—is a few blocks from our house in Seattle. The name? Yoon's Yoga Bliss.

The day before the grand opening of Yoon's Yoga Bliss, I got word that my book had received representation. It felt like our lives and dreams were running parallel, and that even though our missions were different, they supported one another. Both of us were pursuing our dreams with the sole intention of benefiting others through our work.

I started my journey to Korea with the intention of finding my purpose in life and of finding peace. I found both of those things, and more. I found my life partner, who walked beside me and is still walking beside me on this journey, like a great big mirror, reflecting all that I was and all that I am.

As unlikely as our pairing was, I know now that it was meant to be. The heart doesn't follow a rational path, nor does it follow an easy one, but those brave enough to follow it will find much more than they ever bargained for.

About the Author

KATHERINE JENKINS is the author of the popular blog "Lessons from the Monk I Married" (www.lessonsfromthemonk imarried.blogspot.com).

She also teaches English as a Second Language at Edmonds Community College.

When she isn't writing or teaching, she likes to hike, travel, meditate, and practice yoga at Yoon's Yoga Bliss (www.yoonsyoga bliss.com), her husband's yoga studio. Katherine and her husband live in Seattle, Washington.

Acknowledgments

A BOOK IS NEVER the work of one person. There's so much that goes on behind the scenes; it still baffles me to this day. When my husband said, about us, "When the time is right, we will meet the people we are supposed to meet," he was right. And I saw evidence of it again when this project started to take shape. I know the timing was right for this book to be born (and it really did feel like a birth, even though I've never experienced an actual birth), because supporters began to appear in my life unexpectedly, without much effort of my own.

Take this comment, which was posted on my blog in response to my post about my fear of finishing this book:

> Thank you for posting in the midst of these last strokes to the dock. Know that you are not alone for a minute— that you are being carried by a vibrant and ever-expanding circle of admirers, supporters, and students of your own love and wisdom.

To that reader, and to the hundreds of other readers and supporters of my blog, "Lessons from the Monk I Married," I owe the biggest thanks. I seriously don't think there would have been a book without all of you (and you know who you all are) who cheered me on and believed I had something important to say, even when I doubted myself.

And on that note, I am so grateful for the string of people who led me to my wonderful agent. Tara Austin, my college friend, introduced my blog to writer Laura Munson, who in turn connected me to her agent (and now mine) Tricia Davey.

I certainly couldn't have made it this far without the help of freelance editor Ingrid Emerick of Girl Friday Productions. (My husband found out about Ingrid during a private yoga session with Kristin Rowe-Finkbeiner, cofounder of the nationally recognized organization Moms Rising. Ingrid had assisted Kristin in her book-writing process, and Kristin highly recommended her.) Since the beginning of my book journey, Ingrid has been my sounding board, my mentor, my friend, and my cheerleader. Her help has been invaluable.

After hearing so many great things about Tricia through Laura, I jumped the gun and sent her a query letter. I knew that it could take months, even years, to get agent representation, so I didn't think I'd hear back any time soon. But in less than a week, Tricia contacted me and wanted to see the proposal. On a moment's notice, Ingrid got someone to look after her kids while she ran down to the office to put the finishing touches on the proposal, which had been written but was not in the proper format to be sent. We were able to send it off that day.

All I can say is "thank you, thank you, thank you" to this interconnected web of people. It's amazing how I went from "How do I go about getting this thing published?" to "Oh my god! It's going to be published!"

I also have to thank my very lovely agent, Tricia Davey, for that part. She took a risk with me, but she believed I had the "makings of a great book." She sent a round of submissions out, and I got discouraged when we received several rejection letters (they were very positive rejection letters, with some excellent constructive feedback, but I felt dejected nonetheless). Tricia reminded me that this process takes time, that I just had to keep trying and believing. I am so grateful for her encouragement. I reworked the proposal a bit, and in our second round of submissions, we had a few publishing houses who were seriously interested in the book.

Finally, the book found a lovely home at Seal Press, where I was so fortunate to have not just one editor, but *two!* A *big* thank you to publisher Krista Lyons for seeing the potential of this book and for encouraging me when things got overwhelming during the writing process; to Executive Editor Brooke Warner for your careful and consistent editing guidance; and to the entire team at Seal for all your hard work and effort on my book.

A *huge* thank you also goes out to my writing group (Writers Rising, www.writersrising.blogspot.com)—particularly to Deborah Clark-Blome and Lynne Walker, my coworkers, for jumping on board the Writers Rising bandwagon with so much enthusiasm, for holding my hand through this entire journey, and most of all, for *believing!* Thanks to you both and to Debbie Barks for your constructive feedback in the prereading of my book.

Thank you to my best friend, Lena Hillinga Haas, who has stood by me since fourth grade and never doubted my potential to succeed at anything I dared to try; and to my family—they've always believed in me and given me great support.

Deep gratitude goes to my meditation teacher, S. N. Goenka, whose words and teachings have carried me on this path, and who encouraged me, in person, to be strong.

Last, but definitely not least, to my husband: I'm not sure how you did it. I'm not sure how you've been able to calmly stick by me all these years (and particularly through this book journey, which was so trying for me). You've cooked for me, taught yoga to me, meditated with me, listened to me read my book over and over again, and whenever I doubted myself, you shined a light on all that I am and all that I could be. You are my light. I love you, and I'm so very, very grateful to have you right beside me in this journey of life.

Selected Titles from Seal Press

For more than thirty years, Seal Press has published groundbreaking books. By women. For women.

1,000 Mitzvahs: How Small Acts of Kindness Can Heal, Inspire, and Change Your Life, by Linda Cohen. $16.00, 978-1-58005-365-5. When her father passes away, Linda Cohen decides to perform one thousand mitzvahs, or acts of kindness, to honor his memory—and discovers the transformational power of doing good for others.

Found: A Memoir, by Jennifer Lauck. $17.00, 978-1-58005-395-2. Picking up where her NY Times best-selling memoir, *Blackbird*, left off, Jennifer Lauck shares the powerful story of her search for her birth mother, and lays bare the experience of a woman searching for her identity.

Follow My Lead: What Training My Dogs Taught Me about Life, Love, and Happiness, by Carol Quinn. $17.00, 978-1-58005-370-9. Unhappy with her failing love affair, her stagnant career, and even herself,

Carol Quinn enrolls her two Rhodesian ridgebacks into dog agility training—and becomes the "alpha dog" of her own life in the process.

Rocking the Pink: Finding Myself on the Other Side of Cancer, by Laura Roppé. $17.00, 978-1-58005-417-1. The funny, poignant, and inspirational memoir of a woman who took on breast cancer by channeling her inner rock star.

Wanderlust: A Love Affair with Five Continents, by Elisabeth Eaves. $16.95, 978-1-58005-311-2. A love letter from the author to the places she's visited—and to the spirit of travel itself—that documents her insatiable hunger for the rush of the unfamiliar and the experience of encountering new people and cultures.

A Cluttered Life: Searching for God, Serenity, and My Missing Keys, by Pesi Dinnerstein. $17.00, 978-1-58005-310-5. A chronicle of Pesi Dinnerstein's touching, quirky, and often comic search for order and simplicity amid an onslaught of relentless interruptions.

Find Seal Press Online
www.SealPress.com
www.Facebook.com/SealPress
Twitter: @SealPress